Hölderlin and the Consequences

Rüdiger Görner

Hölderlin and the Consequences

An Essay on the German 'Poet of Poets'

Rüdiger Görner
Queen Mary University of London Centre for Anglo-German Cultural Relations
London
UK

ISBN 978-3-476-05817-1   ISBN 978-3-476-05818-8   (eBook)
https://doi.org/10.1007/978-3-476-05818-8

© Springer-Verlag GmbH Germany, part of Springer Nature 2021
This book is a translation of the original German edition „Hölderlin und die Folgen" by Görner, Rüdiger, published by Springer-Verlag GmbH, DE in 2016. The translation was done with the help of artificial intelligence (machine translation by the service DeepL.com). A subsequent human revision was done primarily in terms of content, so that the book will read stylistically differently from a conventional translation. Springer Nature works continuously to further the development of tools for the production of books and on the related technologies to support the authors.
This work is subject to copyright. All rights are reserved by the Publisher, whether the whole or part of the material is concerned, specifically the rights of translation, reprinting, reuse of illustrations, recitation, broadcasting, reproduction on microfilms or in any other physical way, and transmission or information storage and retrieval, electronic adaptation, computer software, or by similar or dissimilar methodology now known or hereafter developed.
The use of general descriptive names, registered names, trademarks, service marks, etc. in this publication does not imply, even in the absence of a specific statement, that such names are exempt from the relevant protective laws and regulations and therefore free for general use.
The publisher, the authors, and the editors are safe to assume that the advice and information in this book are believed to be true and accurate at the date of publication. Neither the publisher nor the authors or the editors give a warranty, expressed or implied, with respect to the material contained herein or for any errors or omissions that may have been made. The publisher remains neutral with regard to jurisdictional claims in published maps and institutional affiliations.

This Palgrave Macmillan imprint is published by the registered company Springer-Verlag GmbH, DE part of Springer Nature.
The registered company address is: Heidelberger Platz 3, 14197 Berlin, Germany

To friends from my time in Tübingen

Contents

"Come! into the Open, Friend!" or: A Word of Introduction for the Anglophone Reader 1

Attuning Recollection. 9

Following Hölderlin, Along the Traces of His Words 15

Hölderlin's Sense of Language 21

Consequences (I): Measuring Hölderlin's Poetic Language-Spaces. 33

Consequences (II): Hölderlin and Homeland ("Heimat") 49

Consequence (III): Hölderlin and the Retrospective Visionary. 63

Hölderlin as a Critic of Culture 69

Thus, Hölderlin Came Amongst the Biographers and Editors 83

Existence and Parataxis: Hölderlin's Controversial Thinking—Adorno *Versus* Heidegger 103

"A Sign We Are, Without Interpretation": An Afterlife in Literary Interpretations 113

"Remembering Floating Hölderlin Towers" or:
Writing Hölderlin.................................. 125

"[…] but soon we will be but a song": Musical
Reflections of Hölderlin............................ 143

Credits with Peter Weiss or: Hölderlin/Scardanelli
as Media Event 155

Literature 161

About the Author

Rüdiger Görner is Professor of German with Comparative Literature at Queen Mary University of London. He is also a writer and critic, Fellow of the German Academy for Language and Poetry and recipient of the Henning Kaufmann Award for German Language (2012) and the Reimar Lüst Award of the Alexander von Humboldt Foundation.

Bibliographic Information of the German National Library

The German National Library records this publication in the German National Bibliography; detailed bibliographical data is available on the internet via http://dnb.d-nb.de

"Come! into the Open, Friend!" or: A Word of Introduction for the Anglophone Reader

The name "Friedrich Hölderlin" stands for—difference. In this essayistic study, various perspectives of this very difference will be examined in respect of its poetic and cultural resonances. After all, "Hölderlin" resonates with something unheard-of in the German language, and indeed European poetry around 1800, and it still resonates today. This poet's name has become a synonym for a poetic language constantly in the making. In his œuvre, verses of unparalleled beauty alternate with verbal and grammatical experiments that take the German language, and perhaps poetry as such, to its limit. When reciting this poetry—and this is how Hölderlin envisaged his works to be communicated—one requires a deep breath; for, often enough, it takes one's breath away in astonishment, for instance when realizing the adventurous nature of Hölderlin's syntax and power of verbal images. As we read it, this poetry keeps growing, as it responds, verse by verse, to what the ancient Greek conception of πνεῦμα entails—at once an organic unfolding of the spirit of nature, divine inspiration coupled with the realization of the potential of language.

This is one side of Hölderlin's poetic legacy. But there is another, and this study will consider both with equal measure. It is the learned poet, acutely aware of what was going on in his time—politically, socially, and intellectually. He observed himself and his own reactions to the fundamental changes that occurred around 1800 without being self-obsessed. To some extent, he found ways to transcend himself through poetry and engage with Antiquity and its curious pointers towards a future world. Hölderlin turned out to be a pre-Socratic poet in modern times, or a pre-modernist as you wish, someone who lived in perpetual anticipation of things to come, which he envisaged as poetic models for a better future.

Hölderlin was, and wanted to be, different in the sense that he saw quite clearly just how unusual, if not anachronistic, his approach to writing poetry and translating from ancient Greek was in his time. He wrote in praise of friendship knowing that loneliness was his lot. Love (for the banker's wife, Susette Gontard, who was also the mother of one of his private tutees,) was his tonic with ultimately poisonous effect. Liberty was the essence of what he took from witnessing the French Revolution from a distance, but confinement was to be his destiny. He yearned for stability but ended up as a perpetual "wanderer" between known and unknown territories. His poetic imagination knew no bounds and his language kept opening new spaces at the risk of breaking up its conventional meaning and means of communication.

He was a poet and took delight in ambiguity and the opaque. He gave expression to the rebellion of his soul and yet marvelled at the ideal of "moderation". His finest play is the drama of his own life, second only to his translation of *Antigone* by Sophocles, arguably the most stunning rendering of a theatrical text from Greek antiquity in German to date.

Hölderlin's hymns and elegies, odes and poetic fragments, constitute a verbal treasure of unprecedented poetic skill and inspiration, but he also wrote one of the finest novels about a political idealist, whom he called Hyperion, whose (Greek) utopia is left in tatters by the end of this narrative in letter-form.

It is tempting to read at least some of Hölderlin's works biographically; for instance his poem *Half of Life* (*Hälfte des Lebens*) is so widely known partly because it seems to contain a self-fulfilling poetic prophecy, for Hölderlin's own life was cut almost exactly in half. He was 73-years old when he died in 1843, thirty-seven years of which he spent in a perpetual state of delusion or "insanity". "Half of Life" with its two strophes, seven lines each, offers what Hölderlin mastered so well: a chillingly beautiful composition, utterly self-contained, the epitome of an entirely balanced "harmonious dissonance" if ever there was one in the German language.

Even though "England" does not feature prominently in Hölderlin's works there is an impressive line-up of English-language poets who engaged with them in the form of translations and adaptations, ranging from Michel Hamburger to Christopher Middleton, David Gascoyne to David Constantine and India Russell. In fact, Hölderlin's own knowledge of English literature was limited. He engaged intensively with Edward Young's *The Complaint: or Night Thoughts* (1742), which influenced his conception of "Nachtgesänge" (Songs of the Night, 1803), most likely in a German version published in 1789. Likewise, he consulted Richard Chandler's *Travels in Asia Minor and Greece;*

or An Account of a Tour, Made at the Expense of the Society of Dilettanti (Oxford 1775/78), again in German translation (Leipzig 1776/77), as a main source for his novel *Hyperion*. Through his familiarity with Klopstock, Hölderlin may have had some knowledge of Milton's *Paradise Lost*. But he was certainly no "Shakespearian" and, in this respect too, was significantly different from most of his literary contemporaries who unreservedly indulged in "Shakesperomania". In his drafts the name "Shakespeare" is only mentioned once but unrelated and of no consequence. The other name on this sheet of paper is "Columbus". Yet, there is no basis for arguing that Hölderlin regarded Shakespeare as the Columbus of the mind, poetry, or drama. But then there is a puzzling reference to "things English" in a most unlikely context, namely his first, though late (1804/05), attempt at writing a hymn on Greece. The passage reads in German: "Gärten wachsen um Windsor. Hoch/Ziehet, aus London,/ Der Wagen des Königs./Schöne Gärten sparen die Jahrzeit./ Am Canal. Tief aber liegt/Das ebene Weltmeer, glühend." ("Gardens are growing around Windsor./The King's carriage passes by from London./Beautiful gardens are saving the season./At the Channel. Deep down lies/The levelled sea of the world, glowingly."). One plausible connection could be that Hölderlin remembered an event that occurred seven years earlier: The heir to the throne of the Dukedom (later, by Napoleon's grace, Kingdom) of Württemberg, Prince Friedrich Wilhelm Karl, got married in London in May 1797 to one of the daughters of King George III, Charlotte Auguste Mathilde; the ensuing celebrations took place at Windsor Castle. For the "subjects" in the relatively small principality of Württemberg, reports about this union between their future ruler and an English-Hanoverian princess would have been a memorable occasion and subject for smalltalk, even though at the time (18 May 1797) our poet from Württemberg, Friedrich Hölderlin, lived "abroad" in Frankfurt/Main as a tutor with the Gontard family and the city was threatened to be overrun by French troops. But would the then rebellious and anti-royal Hölderlin really have bothered about these festivities in London and Windsor given these precarious circumstances? And what about the years 1804/05 when he drafted this hymn, arguably alluding to this event? In December 1804, his friend, Isaak von Sinclair, took part as an official representative of the principality of Homburg, where Hölderlin was by now—pro forma—employed as a Court Librarian, at the coronation of Napoleon in Paris. Only two months later, Sinclair had to stand trial for an attempted plot against the sovereign of Württemberg with traumatic consequences for Hölderlin, who was too close for comfort to the accused conspirators. In this situation he comes up with this surprising reference to "Windsor" as if he had wanted to distract himself from these harsh realities. For once, vision and a vague memory blended together in his typically idealized image of Greece and the dream of the bucolic scenario around Windsor.

This example illustrates just how intrinsic allusions in Hölderlin's poetry can be. In all that testifies to the sheer power of his creative imagination in his highly inspired œuvre there was little that happened by accident. I agree with Charlie Louth when he argues that "most of Hölderlin's poems are concerned with the nature and possibility of transition. Through the complexity of their syntax, the intricate jointing of their rhythms, and their abrupt shifts between images, we are trained in the dynamics of moving through uncertainty, and given experiences of how it can resolve itself into coherence." Indeed, these verbal movements and rhythmic dynamics constitute an almost irresistible momentum; it is both uplifting and suggestive, daring and far-reaching, right into present-day where a renewed belief in the value of words is so much needed. It was therefore not frivolous when a group of young aspiring poets and writers celebrated this poet with a volume full of verbal experiments under the alluring title *Hölderlinks*. For this poet, who shared the year of his birth with Beethoven, Hegel and Wordsworth, with all his aspirations, frustrations and astonishing accomplishments, is truly alive today. Goethe's sibyl, Manto, in the Second Part of his drama *Faust*, could have said to Hölderlin, had she known him better, what she said to the ever-striving protagonist on his way to Greece: "I love those who yearn for the impossible."

This English version of my essay on Hölderlin and his aftermath also represents an essay in translation practices. In the age of *Hölderlinks* it seems not out of place to apply the most advanced digital language techniques to an experiment with translation. Highly sophisticated software programmes facilitated the production of this English version of my examination of Hölderlin, first published in German in 2016. It was in itself the result of a preoccupation with this poet since my student days in Tübingen back in the late 1970s and early 1980s. As it happened, I took "him" with me when I, still a student, came to England in 1981 and soon encountered the very *homme de lettres* who did so much for the comprehensive introduction of Hölderlin's works through his highly accomplished translations, Michael Hamburger. But before meeting him I found myself in extensive conversations with H.G. Adler, a former émigré, survivor of exterminations camps and later their most profound analyst, an eminent writer and poet, who made it plain to me that, in order to understand Hölderlin more fully, I would have to study the works of Friedrich Gottlieb Klopstock. Adler, who had earned his doctorate in the pre-war years from the University of Prague with a thesis on the rhythmical structures and "music" in Klopstock's poetry, turned out to be the ideal *poetic* mentor for this different approach to a poet with whom I believed myself to have been "familiar" already, following my rigorous Hölderlin studies in Tübingen under the direction of the eminent philologist and editor of Hölderlin's works, Jochen Schmidt.

All three would have been aghast at the sheer thought of allowing a "machine" to facilitate translation of this kind. I myself was initially reluctant to consider a proposal made by my reader at Metzler Verlag (Stuttgart), Oliver Schütze, who informed me about this new arrangement with the Nature Publishing Group, including Palgrave Macmillan. But coincidence had it that I had just completed a study on *Bildung im digitalen Zeitalter* (*Education and Cultural Formation in the Digital Age*), very much under the impression of the Corona pandemic, in which I argued in favour of a measured and responsible utilization of virtual environments in educational contexts. This meant that I was somehow prepared for agreeing to subject *Hölderlin und die Folgen* to this experiment with artificial intelligence.

Moreover, it occurred to me that, on reflection, the notion of a somewhat artificial intelligence had begun to germinate in Hölderlin's time already. From the French Materialists of the late eighteenth century to E.T.A. Hoffmann's story about an "automaton" (1814), let alone Mary Shelley's novel *Frankenstein*, eminent writers had suggested the idea of creating simulations of individuals on the basis of a paradox, "organic artificiality". The over-arching question and concern come back to us today with a vengeance and sharply intensified urgency: Is therefore the digital world, with its full implementation and activation of artificial intelligence, the new form of "materialism"? Or is it an expression of a continuing hybridization of artificial and human inputs?

But back to the admittedly smaller, but nonetheless exemplary, case of our book: Even though, initially, *Hölderlin and the Consequences* was to appear under the label book "auto-translation"—the necessary editorial processes made it a blending of artificial intelligence, a human sense of style and human knowledge of contexts—a potent hybrid indeed. Going through what AI provided me with was an experience of a truly special kind. In some cases, the solution found by AI for highly complex phrases was staggeringly ingenious, if this the right word to use in this context, whilst there were (frequent and, dare I say, predictable) instances of complete "misunderstandings" and misconceptions, if there is such a thing as "cognitive comprehension" in the world of digital impulses.

In terms of content, this English version includes references to material that was not available to me back in 2015/16. Most notably, this refers to a poem by the Austrian Expressionist poet, Georg Trakl on Hölderlin, which only came to light in 2016. I offer it in my translation with permission by Hans Weichselbaum of the Trakl Centre in Salzburg. My main thanks go to the copy editor Aishwarya Iyer and project manager Nikita Dhiwar at Springer's for their consideration and patience, and to Oliver Schütze (Metzler Publishers) for his initiative in the first place.

Attuning Recollection

I distinctly remember an evening in May 1991 after closing time on the Zeil, the main shopping mall, in Frankfurt. According to the poster, a puppeteer coming from Jena stows his puppets in a travel bag and counts his coins. Drunken people surround a bronze sculpture; meanwhile young people with or without tattoos and mohawks jeer on their roller skates.

Then the Katharinenkirche opens its doors. Not far from here, the Gontards lived in the Palais *Weißer Hirsch* am Großen Hirschgraben, where Hölderlin held his second tutor position, at a time when Goethe's mother still lived in the neighbourhood, as did the poetess Karoline von Günderrode and, for a time, Hegel. A queue quickly forms in front of the box office at the church portal. One of the visitors asks whether there is a reduced entrance fee for dropouts; those standing in line acknowledge this with a tired laugh.

In the Katharinenkirche, which has been cleared out except for a few rows of benches at the sides, plastic sheeting covers the floor, steps, altar and organ. Chorus ladies appear behind the altar. In the middle of the church, an actor taking the part of Friedrich Hölderlin's protagonist Hyperion crouches and tells of his youth, his upbringing as an idealist, his love and how it was transformed into an insatiable longing for the unattainable. The chorus ladies, half Muses, half Erynnia, comment on Hyperion's life and failure.

Some glowing evening light falls through the colourful church windows, enhanced by the mirrored glass of the bank skyscrapers all around. One hears a dreamily sounding bell, as if it vaguely remembers the passing time.

Hyperion plays his youth, Diotima her own, wrapped in plastic foil. They thus appear clothed and exposed at the same time, strong and vulnerable. The sacred space is transformed into a place of sacrifice, that is to say, love and (political) ideal, hope and faith are to form a new religion. What remains is the feeling of futility and irritation. "This is how I came to be among the Germans" ("So kam ich unter die Deutschen"), Hyperion argues, played in Frankfurt by a Turk named Ömer. He says what is not in the text, but could be: "WE ALWAYS HAVE ONE FOOT IN THE DOOR."

Then he calls *Diotima* several times, although she is standing next to him. They try to hug, reach into the void, and in doing so move further and further apart. *Diotima*. The lover turned into a pseudonym. Of course, she was not allowed to be called by her real name *Susette Gontard* in the novel. And Hölderlin could only be Hyperion. But just how much trouble had Hölderlin gone to in order to separate Diotima from Susette and Hyperion from himself, I wonder. Could the work on the novel cancel out his desire or did it increase it? And what did she, Susette, feel when reading *Hyperion?* We do not know, and will never know the decisive thing. *To whom else but you*—has there ever been more intimate a dedication than this incomplete sentence? Hölderlin included it in the second volume of his *Hyperion in* 1799, which hardly anyone wanted to take note of at the time, despite the publisher's eager efforts. *To whom else but you.*

But why these foils in the church room, which are otherwise only seen during renovation work? Are they supposed to generate the contours of the real flow, just as Hyperion perceived his world in Hölderlin's novel? His idealism prevents him from recognizing the true character of his environment. Hyperion's strength of feeling and enthusiasm rob him of reflection, and thus of his sense of the possible. His visionary farsightedness stands in the way of real insight. Hyperion finally becomes a disillusioned seeker. And yet hope prevails in the end: "As the discord of lovers, so are the dissonances of the world. Reconciliation is in the midst of strife, and all that is separated is found again." ("Wie der Zweist der Liebenden, sind die Dissonanzen der Welt. Versöhnung ist mitten im Streite, und alles Getrennte findet sich wieder.")

Even the deranged poet could still beat his "little table" with his hand when he quarrelled—"with his thoughts," as Lotte Zimmer passed on, according to her future lodger, Ernst Friedrich Wyneken.

Nothing can be more deceptive than wanting to *invoke* Hölderlin. His poetry sanctions nothing we do today. But what it "endows", or "stiftet", to use one of Hölderlin's poignant words, is the requirement to deal with an unheard-of language, or to put it differently: with what is possible in the German language in terms of poetic outrageousness.

An anthology along the lines of "Through the Year with Hölderlin" would be nonsensical, no matter how many poems he wrote about sowing and reaping, summer and winter, homecoming and farewell. For these poems are not companions along the way, but a dizzying balancing act for every reader.

"What is it that/About those ancient blessed shores/ Holds me so in its thrall/I love her more than my own native land?" ("Was ist es, das/An die alten seligen Küsten/ Mich fesselt, dass ich mehr noch/Sie liebe, als mein Vaterland?") Not infrequently, we are tempted to answer Hölderlin's questions, and join him in asking such questions. But do we still have the certainty to join him in saying: "But where the danger is, also grows the saving power" ("Wo aber Gefahr ist, wächst/Das Rettende auch")? Would we have been hymnal enough to be able to proclaim in the spirit of his *Celebration of Peace (Friedensfeier)* with a good conscience and a free heart: "… but soon we shall be song" ("… bald sind wir aber Gesang")?

Should we really conjure up Hölderlin's contemporaneity? Or is it only left to us to ascertain his strangeness? When the poet was commemorated on the hundredth anniversary of his death, in 1943, there was a "Reich celebration", with wreaths from the "Führer" and paladins simulating their education, with the "Schicksalslied" (song of fate) set to music by Johannes Brahms and an unmentionable speech by the first president of the Hölderlin Society appointed by the Reich Governor, the "poet" Gerhard Schumann (whose name, for the sake of literature, must be immediately forgotten). In this ghostly way, barely a quarter of a year after the battle of Stalingrad, Hölderlin was to be appropriated ideologically. But take the trouble to read up on how—despite all the concessions to the *Zeitgeist* of Fascism and the expectations of the party officials weighing on them—Paul Kluckhohn and the young Friedrich Beißner nevertheless endeavoured to create a differentiated image of Hölderlin in their two memorial lectures on 7 June 1943. One year later, another Hölderlin admirer followed the poet's call for a "bolder word" with the boldest possible action, an attempt on Hitler's life: Claus Schenk Graf von Stauffenberg.

All troubles with the German fatherland, even the problems of unification and the so-called refugee crisis, could easily be adorned with quotations from Hölderlin. But Hölderlin's presence is not based on the fact that we can extract pieces from his poetry. He is present through his struggle for coherence in a torn world. His determination to give expression to his will to completion in his poetic compositions is truly moving and even noticeable in his fragments.

Following Hölderlin, Along the Traces of His Words

Sometime between 1803 and 1805: Hölderlin translates some of Pindar's fragments and writes emphatically idiosyncratic notes on them. They deal with a great variety of subjects, such as wisdom, truth and tranquillity, age, infinity, divinity and the dolphin, asylums and what can enliven, or invigorate, existence. They are poetic and discursive echoes of his Pindar translations of 1800, an Olympic anthem and Pythian odes. In retrospect, these translations read like rehearsals of what will be called Hölderlin's late work, the great hymns, worked according to the Pindar model in the sense of an "imitatio Pindari", which had already gone out of fashion at the time. Yet Pindar had been in great demand for more than two centuries, ever since Ronsard's *Odes Pindariques* (1550), the English "Pindaricks" of the 17th century, Opitz's proclamation "O meine Lust/ Pindarisieren" ("O my Desire,/To write in a Pindarian mode"), Klopstock's and Herder's enthusiasm for this model, which was as classical as it was random. The model

Hölderlin used was at the highest level of philological research of the time: The 1798 Pindar edition of Christian Gottlob Heyne, the founder of modern antiquity studies.

Hölderlin can only be understood inadequately if one does not take into account from the outset his turning to Greek culture, especially to Sophocles and Pindar, but also to Sappho. Antiquity and modernity "tore" at him, to use one of his favourite words from that time. He exposed himself to both with a determination that was unusual even in relation to the German enthusiasm for Greece. In a letter dated 4 December 1801, he writes

I have laboured long on it and know now that aside from that which must be the supreme thing for the Greeks and for us, namely the living relation and the skill, we ought not to have anything in common with them.
But that which is one's own has to be learned just as well as that which is foreign. For this reason, the Greeks are indispensable to us. Only we will not catch up with them precisely in that which is our own, in the national meaning of the word, because, as I said, the free use of that which is one's own is the most difficult.

(Ich habe lange daran laboriert und weiß nun daß außer dem, was bei den Griechen und uns das höchste sein muß, nemlich dem lebendigen Verhältnis und Geschick, wir nicht wohl etwas *gleich* mit ihnen haben dürfen.
Aber das eigene muß so gut gelernt sein, wie das Fremde. Deswegen sind uns die Griechen unentbehrlich. Nur werden wir ihnen gerade in unserem Eigenen, Nationellen nicht nachkommen, weil wie gesagt, der *freie* Gebrauch des *Eigenen* das schwerste ist.)

Labouring and—possibly in vain—*learning*. He had tried out the pedagogical methods as a tutor—in Waltershausen and Frankfurt, in Hauptwil, and soon after in Bordeaux. His being a tutor had also put him to the test. But he failed to pass these tests. The "free use of what belongs to oneself"—a concept central to Hölderlin's poetry as well as his life—became more important to him, no matter how hard he tried to provide a liberal education for his private pupils.

In the *Third Pythian Ode* of Pindar Hölderlin translated: "Small in the small, great in the great/I want to be; but the demon when talking around/I want to exercise with my senses/thus honouring fate". ("Klein im Kleinen, Groß im

Großen/Will ich sein; den umredenden aber immer mit Sinnen/Den Dämon will ich üben nach meinem/Ehrend dem Geschick.") What may have interested him in this Pindar passage? Possibly the preservation of human measures as well as the value of the senses. But did this "demon" allow himself to be "exercised" or educated? The demon also "tore" at him, exposing him to inner tensions that were increasingly difficult to overcome: "Do you know the root of all my evil? I want to live the art to which my heart is attached, and yet I must work among men […]". ("Weißt Du die Wurzel alles meines Übels? Ich möchte der Kunst leben, an der mein Herz hängt, und ich muß mich herumarbeiten unter den Menschen […].")

But the key Pindarian words, and even more so Hölderlin's comments on them, show that this "working among people" was quite important to him. In a letter to his (half) brother, later an administrative officer, viticulture expert and antiquity researcher, Karl Gok, Hölderlin calls the "German character" a "tremendous fallow field" that had to be "ploughed over" by writing political speeches, for example, about "the lack of a sense of nature among scholars and businessmen, about religious slavery", about "guilds, city rights, communal rights".

"How are things in your political world?" ("Wie geht es denn in Euer politischen Welt?"), he asks in the same letter of March 1798, and in November of that year, together with his even more politically radical friend, Isaak von Sinclair, he will visit the Congress of Rastatt, where the representatives of the Swabian estates were to present the project of a Swabian republic. Four years later, the two friends meet again at the Regensburg Reichstag where the Reichsdeputationshauptschluss (Main Resolution of the Imperial Deputation) brought about the self-abolition of the Holy Roman Empire and with it the abolition of the privileges of empire-free cities. It is not known how Hölderlin reacted to this. But his interest in the life of the ancient polis is well known; it is likely that in Frankfurt he got to know the way of life in an imperial city, which was a kind of transfer of this ancient model. Hölderlin's political consciousness may have been reflected in his desire to work publicly through poetry as a poetic educator, a poet who thinks and feels ahead. (His great hymn **Friedensfeier** [*Celebration of Peace*]—a reaction to the Peace of Lunéville of February 1801, which ended the Second Coalition War against France and enabled Napoléon to annex the left bank of the Rhine—had, according to the preface, originally been intended by him as a poetic pamphlet). But this wish was countered by the bitter realisation that his countrymen were ignoring him. Before he goes to Bordeaux, he confesses to his friend Casimir von Böhlendorff in one of his most shattering letter passages in the letter of 4 December 1801:

Parting is all I can think now. It's been a long time since I have cried. But it cost me bitter tears when I decided to leave my fatherland, perhaps for good. For what is more dear to me in this world? But they have no use for me. Still, I shall and must remain German, even if the needs of my heart – and belly – drive me all the way to Tahiti.

(Ich bin jetzt voll Abschieds. Ich habe lange nicht geweint. Aber es hat mich bittre Tränen gekostet, da ich mich entschloß, mein Vaterland noch jetzt zu verlassen, vielleicht auf immer. Denn was hab' ich lieberes auf der Welt? Aber sie können mich nicht brauchen. Deutsch will und muß ich übrigens bleiben, und wenn mich die Herzens- und die Nahrungsnot nach Otaheiti triebe.)

Intimately acquainted with the intellectual currents of his time, Pietism and Jacobinism, Kantianism and Rousseauism, the constitutional structure of Switzerland and certain plans for an overthrow in Hesse-Homburg and Württemberg, Hölderlin was, however, also anxious to emancipate himself from his political consciousness for the sake of safeguarding "purity" for his poetry. Hölderlin admitted (to himself): "In the end, it is true that the less man learns or knows about the state—regardless of its shape and form—the freer he is". ("Am Ende ist es doch wahr, je weniger der Mensch vom Staat erfährt und weiß, die Form sei, wie sie will, um desto freier ist er.") Or in the language of the Pindar fragments: "And think differently in another time." ("Und anderes denk in anderer Zeit.")

One of the translated fragments is about "asylum". Hölderlin calls asylums "places of rest", places where God and man meet and "recognize each other". The restless man finds a hold in the asylum. There justice prevails, because Themis, Zeus' wife, whom Hölderlin expressly calls "orderly", gave birth to the "Asylum". The asylum is therefore a holy place, which must be respected.

What was that supposed to mean? It suggests that the level of a humane (and therefore civil) society also depends on *how* it guarantees and implements the right to asylum. In the sense of Pindar and Hölderlin, asylum is understood as a polis within the polis, as the heart of a value-oriented state, as a haven of peace in times of radical change. Asylum is the place of practiced altruism and thus sheer humanism.

Following Hölderlin means tracking down such surprising areas in his work. As it happened, he himself was eventually in need of an "asylum" and found it with a master carpenter from Tübingen, who took care of him and who passed this spirit of care on to his daughter, who looked after Hölderlin until his death in 1843.

But they do not need me—before you think about the consequences of his poetic work, this line of Hölderlin's can haunt one. Yet he wanted so much to be *needed*—whether as a friend or tutor, as an educator of "his" Germans and a renewer of their and his own language. What more did he want than to belong somehow, even if he himself was probably never quite clear to whom or what.

Hölderlin or the poetics of being superfluous—this could be the title of a study on the poet. For no one before Hölderlin has experienced the idea of the "superfluous human being" as tantalisingly as he did, with the possible exception of Jakob Reinhold Michael Lenz, who repeatedly found himself in the situation of having to re-live and recreate what Goethe, his friend and rival, had experienced—including Goethe's Sesenheim love affair with Friederike Brion. After Hölderlin, it was Ivan S. Turgenev who, in the *Diary of a Superfluous Man* (1850), literally shaped this feeling into a sign of modernity.

Picking up the track of Hölderlin's language means following his verbal traces: What would they consist of? Words such as: Love, Gods, eccentric path, centre, calculation, thunderstorm, not to forget the conjunction "but" that introduces an opposition or reversal? Hölderlin formed his poetic essentialism from them. He wanted to track it down, the (sacred) essence of the word, in the sense of getting to the bottom of every word. George Steiner was to call this Hölderlin's "ontology of language", which had already found its justification in Martin Heidegger's works on Hölderlin. No poet has ever been granted such afterthoughts on his poetic words, or verbal material, at least not with such intensity—whether to the advantage or disadvantage of the effect of this poetry, can hardly be determined. Yet Heidegger's approach to Hölderlin remains so idiosyncratic that it will have to be considered here as a special episode.

As the "poet of poets" and an advocate of the poetic, Hölderlin continues to have consequences for our understanding of linguistic-artistic translation, too. The intrinsic value of his achievements as a translator was recognized and appreciated relatively late, in the case of his *Antigone* translation by Bertolt Brecht in his *Arbeitsjournal* of 1942. Also, and especially as a translator, Hölderlin favoured the "principle of literalism", which led him to form "word-for-word metaphrases" (George Steiner), bringing him closer to classical Greek in German than any other translator.

Hölderlin's Sense of Language

Hölderlin avoided nothing more than the insignificant, meaningless word. His poetry reads like an intervention against banality; he even felt he had to weigh his own punctuation marks, as it were, before using them.

But how would a language be found to correspond to Hölderlin's poetry in order to appreciate it critically? How to approach this unique poetic language without falling into the rhapsodic and succumbing to the pathos of the sublime? Can one pay justice to this work sufficiently with the help of critical philology, or only if one (additionally) draws on everything that the arsenal of literary studies and its methods has to offer? Does the biographical research on Hölderlin, which at times attempts to tune into his life on an equal footing with him—by narrating in the manner of Peter Härtling, for example, or attempting to transform him into a simulation with Pierre Bertaux, help us? Should we wander like Hölderlin did from Nürtingen to Bordeaux following in the poet's footsteps of 1801 whilst trying to recapture his sense of utter desolation, or re-enact the love story of Hölderlin and Susette Gontard in order to refine our understanding of his work, or shall we limit ourselves completely to him as his own artistic figure, to Scardanelli, whom he allowed himself to become, as Peter Schünemann and—more emphatically poetic—Friederike Mayröcker have done? These questions continue to occupy anyone who attempts to write on this poet.

Martin Walser called this poet of poets "contagious", even spoke of the "dangerousness of the Hölderlin sound". Hölderlin's rhetoric is an enigma and suggestive of an enigmatic magic. Neither references to Pindar, nor to Klopstock, and not even to Schiller are sufficient to adequately explain the poetic event with the name "Hölderlin", and his treatment of verse and words. With him, with his poetic treatment of language, the sublime was redefined in German—even in Hölderlin's sketches and fragments; a sublime that one looks up to, and shudders before in sheer amazement.

Hölderlin stands for the extraordinary in the German language. And what his "very last poems" are about, which he used to sign with the phrase "with subservience/Scardanelli" and seemingly fictitious data, which have never been deciphered, remains appropriately open. They are poems, which he produced allegedly in an automatic fashion dedicated to the seasons, a particular "prospect", "higher forms of life" and "higher humanity". They rhyme in a half witty, half naïve manner; they repeat motifs as if it were an attempt at litanical self-assurance. In one of his even more litany-like letters to his mother from the late period, Hölderlin stated a point that surprisingly reads like a (seemingly) rational and decidedly impersonal justification for these absurd-looking utterances in letter-form: "The repetition of what one has written is not always an unnecessary quality. It is founded in what we are talking about, that when one exhorts oneself to do good and says something serious to oneself, it is not taken very badly if one says the same thing and does not always put forward something that is not ordinary". ("Das Wiederholen von dem, was man geschrieben hat, ist nicht immer eine unnötige Beschaffenheit. Es ist in dem, wovon die Rede ist, gegründet, daß, wenn man sich zum Guten ermahnt, und sich etwas Ernstliches sagt, es nicht sehr übel genommen wird, wenn man eben dasselbe sagt, und nicht immer etwas vorbringt, das nicht gewöhnlich ist.") Were these lines written by a mentally deranged person or by someone who was still sure of his stylistic possibilities? Hölderlin's sentence, which testifies to linguistic differentiation, could be paraphrased as follows: "Self-promotion of the good and serious justifies the autosuggestion generated by linguistic repetition of simple insights." Repetition with moral intent—that was one side of this Hölderlinian self-protection against the ever-present threat of self-loss. He apparently no longer wanted to be challenged by incriminating complexities and eccentricities. The sublime pathos of the past, the art of inversion and the enormous cadences in his language were revoked in this sentence to his mother. The last, always dateless, letters to his mother resemble invocations of the simple, the unpretentious.

The anachronistic dates that Hölderlin gave to his latest poems, probably written between 1810 and 1843, range from 1648 to 1940, from 1748/1758, his favourite years, to 1871, which points on the one hand to a schizophrenic relationship to time and on the other to a markedly playful approach to time. One could also say that Hölderlin wanted to experiment with time, to specify dates for his attempts at de-temporalization, with the aim of giving an exact date for the departure from time. A more paradoxical relationship to time would hardly be conceivable.

But there is something else: by dating his poems in this way, Hölderlin created spaces of time, evoking the future

1871 and 1940, as well as the past: 1648. If one adds to this the principle of repetition, which he used excessively after 1806, then the assumption is indeed obvious that Hölderlin could have seen a special value in the time-embracing faculty of verbal utterance, precisely after his so-called derangement.

Words have a specific, unexpected effect or simply fade away; they break the silence and fall back into it. According to Hölderlin, words can be "deadly factual" ("tödtlichfactisch"), i.e., it can destroy, or "speak more holy", as long as it is "bolder" than the conventional word spoken along these lines.

The word is capable of evoking *and* appeasing the "unheard-of". It can even express the "One that differs in itself", that principle of Heraclitus' thinking that was particularly important to Hölderlin and that his Hyperion had considered to be the most meaningful form of thinking.

Hölderlin regarded language as a "product of creative reflection" ("Product schöpferischer Reflexion"), whereby reflection had always been an aesthetic process; he spoke of the "beautiful reflection" with its *modus experimendi* in the field of verbal art.

In a letter addressed to Schiller in September 1799, Hölderlin coined the expression "magical play of colours of language" to describe the peculiar effect the revered poet's early drama *The Conjuration of Fiesco of Genova (Die Verschwörung des Fiesco von Genua)* had on him. One recalls the words of his Diotima, handed down by Hyperion, which described the appearance of something "like the colours that tremble before our eyes when we look long into the sun". (II, 85) In order to interpret the complex meaning of this expression, reference needs to be made to Hölderlin's detailed letter to his brother in January of the same year, in which he denied the playful character of "true poetry", since, unlike play, it does not merely "disperse", but allows man to gather through it.

Thus, for Hölderlin, the "magical play of colours of language" ("magischen Farbenspiele der Sprache") is not an unproblematic value judgement. For on the one hand, he too strove in his poetry to achieve a dazzling effect of language, but on the other, he did not want to reduce it to the purely playful or merely rhetorical, however "magical" its effect might be. Moreover, the letter to Schiller is striking in that Hölderlin concerns himself specifically with compositional questions concerning the "inner structure" of a poetic work of art. His aphoristic reflections from the Frankfurt period show how precisely he considered the linguistic-syntactic possibilities:

One has inversions of the words in the syntactic period. But then the inversion of the periods themselves must also be greater and more effective. The logical position of the periods, where the reason [of the basic period] is followed by the becoming, the becoming by the goal, the goal by the end, and the secondary propositions are always attached to the back of the main propositions to which they first refer, - is certainly only very rarely useful to the poet.

(Man hat Inversionen der Worte in der Periode. Größer und wirksamer muß aber dann auch die Inversion der Perioden selbst seyn. Die logische Stellung der Perioden, wo dem Grunde (der Grundperiode) das Werden, dem Werden das Ziel, dem Ziele der Zweck folgt, und die Nebensäze immer nur hinten angehängt sind an die Hauptsäze worauf sie sich zunächst beziehen, - ist dem Dichter gewiß nur höchst selten brauchbar.)

Johann Georg Hamann had already drawn attention to the importance of inversions (changes in the construction of the period, i.e. of the sentence, for example verb before subject): "The German language is by its nature capable of these inversions before others; and its boldness contributes to the prestige of our poetic style of writing." Moreover, Hamann pointed out that "the inversion is not simply arbitrary or accidental, but is subject to the judgment of understanding and hearing." Logic of language and feeling for language must therefore work together to form inversions at the right place.

Hölderlin's "bolder word" ("kühnere Wort") almost demanded changes in syntax in order to develop more freely because it was emancipated from conventional syntactic structures. The calculus, which is mentioned several times in his poetic remarks on the Sophoclesian tragedies he translated: *Oedipus* and *Antigone*, must become one with the "boldness" of his expression. In other words: Hölderlin's language did not want to be a "magical play of colours", but a hard-edged prism *and* a melodic structure that vibrates within itself.

The "word" and "language" became central motifs in Hölderlin's poetic work at a time when writing poetry had become more of a laborious process, which is reflected in the increasingly numerous drafts and preliminary stages to poems after 1797/98. Hölderlin repeatedly asked himself one question: Should language enable a purifying pronunciation of the self or, to put it differently, can it only be justified in a "purified" form?

This posed another problem for him: Can language be a suitable means of communication and thus "create" a supporting conversation? In the autumn of 1798, he read the following in a letter from Susette Gontard: "[…] but I cannot express what is right, it remains buried deep in my heart, only tears of melancholy can say that, and then quench them again." ("[…] das Rechte kann ich aber nicht ausdrücken, es bleibt tief in meinem Herzen begraben, nur Thränen der Wehmuth können daß sagen, und wieder stillen.") How would one be able to express what is inside of oneself without distortion? Hölderlin touched on this question a year later in a letter to his mother dated 16 November 1799: "If my inner self never quite arrives at a clear and detailed language, just as much depends on happiness, then I know what I have wanted […]." ("Sollte auch mein Innres nie recht zu einer klaren und ausführlichen Sprache kommen, wie man dann hierinn viel vom Glük abhängt, so weiß ich, was ich gewollt habe [...].") Even before that, he had already found it a torment to have to surrender his feelings to the compulsion to express them in words, as can be seen from a letter to his friend Neuffer in February 1797: "It is also always a death to our silent bliss if it has to be brought to verbal expression." ("Es ist auch immer ein Tod für unsere stille Seligkeit, wenn sie zur Sprache werden muß.")

In his elegy *Homecoming* (*Heimkunft*), Hölderlin then speaks of the fact that the "singer" must ultimately bear the care of the appropriate word, the appropriate expression, alone. In view of this "care", the poet's conversation can only be a soliloquy, or, more precisely, a conversation with language.

That this discourse *with* language is also endangered is shown by the first verses of the draft for the hymn *Mnemosyne,* probably written at the end of 1803: "A sign we are, uninterpreted/Painless are we and have almost/Lost the language in a foreign land" ("Ein Zeichen sind wir, deutungslos/Schmerzlos sind wir und haben fast/Die Sprache in der Fremde verloren."). A more radical reduction cannot be found elsewhere in Hölderlin's work: the names, the words seem to disintegrate into mere sounds and letters, according to Hamann "pure forms a priori, in which nothing belonging to the sensation or concept of an object is encountered". This loss of speech is not "absolute"; however, the most important word in these verses is "almost". The lack of interpretation and sensation of the "sign" can thus be overcome, provided that it is possible to understand this "sign" as a "true aesthetic element" (Hamann) and to recognize the substance of a new knowledge and reason. Thus, the partial loss of language in the "foreign" would be important in order to create new expressive values with a limited supply of signs. Moreover, since "we" are as yet "uninterpreted", others can interpret us. Man as a semiotic phenomenon can be a "sign" for many things—for what exactly remains open to interpretation.

However, Hölderlin had already expressed in his *Hyperion* that the experience of speech loss can also be positive and a prerequisite for a new creation of speech: "For a long time we stood in a state of self-forgetful contemplation, and no one knew what happened to him, until finally too much joy piled up in me and my lost speech began again in tears and sounds of delight [...]." ("Lange standen wir so in holder selbstvergessener Betrachtung, und keines wußte, wie ihm geschah, bis endlich der Freude zu viel in mir sich häufte und in Thränen und Lauten des Entzükens auch meine verlorne Sprache wieder begann [...].") With these words Hyperion recalls his and Diotima's experience of being, heightened in love, and finally their finding of adequate language together.

In the second version of the ode to "*Encouragement*" ("*Ermunterung*"), it becomes clear that expressing oneself is not limited to a subjective concern. The concluding verse refers to a transcendental dimension: "And he who acts without speech preparing/The future without being known, the God, the Spirit/In the word of man, on the good day/Coming years, like before, speaks out". ("Und er, der sprachlos waltet und unbekannt/Zukünftiges bereitet, der Gott, der Geist/Im Menschenwort, am schönen Tage/Kommenden Jahren, wie einst, sich ausspricht.") Hölderlin had already emphasized the speechless work of God in his hexameter hymn *The Archipelagus*: "Silent is the delphic god [...]"; "Silent is the god [...]". ("Stumm ist der delphische Gott [...]"; "Stilleweilend der Gott [...]".) Only a soul "silently united" in the "freer song", as Hölderlin wrote, could serve this God. The ode *Encouragement,* however, also points to the future potential of this interplay between divine speechlessness and silence. Provided that man speaks his language responsibly, he keeps his word ready for the moment when (a) God wants to reveal himself again through language.

In order to be able to "prepare" his own language in this way, man must be able to understand the "silence of the ether", as Hölderlin said in his poem *Da ich ein Knabe war (When I was a boy)*. Moreover, nature, recognized as divinely interwoven, must have taught him: "I was raised by the sound of the purring grove and learned to love among the flowers." ("Mich erzog der Wohllaut/Des säuselnden Hains/Und lieben lernt' ich/Unter den Blumen.") Hölderlin regarded the ether as the unity of physical phenomena such as electricity, magnetism and light, as he may have learned from his demonstrable occupation with Samuel Thomas Sömmerring's study *On the Organ of the Soul* (1796). However, for the poet as such the ether also became a fluid medium of mood.

In the elegy *Bread and Wine (Brod und Wein)*, Hölderlin also established a connection between words and flowers: If man calls "his dearest", then "words, like flowers, must be created for it". What is remarkable about this turn of phrase is that the flowering words can "develop" apparently independently of the speaker. But by naming his dearest real language is not yet created. The naming of something special causes language to form itself automatically—just as plants reproduce. This "organic" form of language formation ensures, provided one follows Hölderlin's train of thought, that the words are not alienated from divine nature, but remain a medium of potential mediation between God and man. Precisely for this reason, what the "mediator" Christ pronounced was *true* language.

Hölderlin's understanding of words may have been one of the reasons why his most important poems, in which he had undoubtedly referred to what was "dearest" to him, often exist in several versions: What was once addressed literally continued to "bloom" or produced new impulses.

But this also implies that Hölderlin's language does not simply bring the designated into existence. It "provides the thing" not only with being, to use Heidegger's phrase, but also enables it to develop further.

The peculiarity of Hölderlin's relationship to language results from his "harmonious" opposition of linguistic logic (in the case of his poetological drafts) and the dynamics of poetic inspiration ("thunderstorm"). For him, prescriptive poetics and a sense of genius were not contradictory. Consciousness of form and willingness to go to the limits of syntax as well as to experiment with words and meaning ("And it sounded Roman what the mountain peak was bulging out…" ["Und Römisches tönend ausbeuget der Spitzberg."]) had been the two sides of his "poetic vocation" as the title of one of his poems reads.

"I never understood the words of man" ("Der Menschen Worte verstand ich nie"), Hölderlin used this verse to characterize the starting point of his poetic work. The failure to understand others led Hölderlin to create his own world of language, in which he could communicate.

How conscious Hölderlin remained of this peculiar precondition of his poetry is demonstrated by the short preface to his great hymn *Friedensfeier (Celebration of Peace)* (ca. 1802/03), in which he writes: "If, however, some find such language too unconventional, I must confess to them: I cannot help it" ("Sollten aber dennoch einige eine solche Sprache zu wenig konventionell finden, so muß ich ihnen gestehen: ich kann nicht anders."). With Lutheran emphasis he professes his way of writing poetry. The following sentence is no less significant: "On a beautiful day, almost any kind of song can be heard, and nature, from which it originated, takes it back" ("An einem schönen Tage läßt sich ja fast jede Sangart hören, und die Natur, wovon es her ist, nimmts auch wieder."). The "beautiful day" probably refers to the Paris Peace Festival of 14 July 1801; the people who are in a good mood as a result are more inclined, the poet hopes, to accept his special style of language as a specific expression of poetic enthusiasm. Moreover, he emphasizes that "almost every style of [poetic] singing", including his own, lies within the range of the "naturally" given linguistic possibilities and is therefore understandable despite its peculiarities, provided that one is willing to engage with it.

His letters from that time expose an issue that had become desperately important to him: as much as he knew how "peculiar" his language was, as little did he understand "the words of men", even though he himself wanted to be understood. "Patriotic and natural, in fact original", he desired to "sing", he wrote to his friend Casimir von Böhlendorff at the end of 1802, convinced that through him "the mode of lyrical speech, or *Sangart,* would take on a different character" in German. The particular style was apparently supposed to become common property, just as the particular style of Sophocles would significantly influence Greek language. This means that Hölderlin worked on the possibility of language's after-effect. His language was intended to have "consequences" more than anything else.

For Hölderlin, language was both material and reason for existence. A one-sidedly existentialist interpretation of his language along Heidegger's lines of argument can therefore do him only partial justice, as will be discussed later. The same must apply to a purely philological and stylistically critical analysis of language. For, as aware as Hölderlin was of the effect of ancient metrical-rhythmical structures, he calculated that the sudden onset of anti-rhythmical periods made the listening reader aware that the unforeseen could always occur, even "in the middle of a word". For example, in *Friedensfeier* (*Celebration of Peace*), when the high-pitched tone breaks off with the following two verses: "Oh! but darker shaded, in the middle of the word, you/terribly deciding a deadly fate." ("Ach! Aber dunkler umschattete, mitten im Wort, dich/Furchtbarentscheidend ein tödlich Verhängnis.") What this fate consists of, however, eludes language; it refers, especially in Hölderlin's late hymns, again and again to the unspeakable.

For Hölderlin, work on language included understanding of silence. The large-scale poem *Friedensfeier (Celebration of peace)* also exposes this connection, almost imploringly: "The principle of fate is that all experience each other,/That when silence is reversed, there is also a language." ("Schiksaalgesez ist diß, daß Alle sich erfahren,/Daß, wenn die Stille kehrt, auch eine Sprache sei.")

With this it is claimed that silence can "turn", that is, it can turn around and need not be final. Furthermore, a positive "fatality" given by fate can be assumed, which is not "fatal", but has linguistically creative effects. Upon man this fate has "imposed" a community-related self-experience; this is not a contradiction in itself but a condition of real conversation. Language, thus, proves to be the other side of silence.

What is it, then, that remains of what the poet could "endow"—conscious of his fate? Certainly not a mere "play of verbal colours" that one merely marvels at, but the task of constantly interpreting the "password", as it is called in *Patmos*, and likewise not to interpret the "fixed letter" arbitrarily, but to "cultivate" it. This means to use language's aesthetic quality creatively and *at the same time* respecting it as a sign of the human. As an "endowing" poet, Hölderlin felt that he had a duty to speak, which included thinking about the consequences of words.

Consequences (I): Measuring Hölderlin's Poetic Language-Spaces

One of Hölderlin's modes of writing, and of feeling, was that of a returning person. "Do the cranes return to you", *the Archipelagus* asks. And Hölderlin himself, time and again, finds his way back to Nürtingen, to his family, returns from the vastness of the world to the narrowness of his home, only to flee it again. All that happens is for the sake of remembrance, which occurs in the mode of return or homecoming. Hölderlin, thus followed an insight of the Roman rhetoric teacher Quintilian, who claimed in his *Institutiones oratoriae:*

Because when we return to any place after a certain time, we not only recognize the place itself, but we also remember what we did there, people come back to us, sometimes even the thoughts that we had made there, return to our minds.

By increasingly using the names of places and countries in his poems and drafts, especially *after* his return from Bordeaux (1802), Hölderlin evoked their auratic memory and cultural richness, which can be shared through these poems. Such locations become poetic cells, as it were, that often grow associatively into lyrical structures, tamed, curtailed by the specifications of the chosen (or imposed) form. In Hölderlin's poetry, places create occasions for memory and expectation, contemplation and imagination, arrival and departure. The "modes of time" (Ernst Cassirer) and those of sensation intertwine. Smyrna and Ephesus, the Caucasus and Palmyra, become fixed or focal points of a longing that can hardly be defined more precisely, but from which the poetic ego must also take leave again, considering its own restrictive living conditions.

In Hölderlin's poetic development, there is a striking tendency towards the poetically expansive, and towards becoming comprehensive in poetic expression. Word, verse and stanza, free rhythms in particular, want to become expansive in his work, but also explore historical periods. One could say he poetically occupied the space *between* earth and heaven. And he won this "land" from the sea of silence. Whatever sound he heard, he was able to integrate into his great project, which proved impossible to complete. He did not have to say, as Faust did with his reclaiming of land from the sea by doubtful, if not criminal, means: "The little bell rings, and I rage"; for Hölderlin raged most against himself, but at least after temporarily believing that he had found "solid ground" and a "permanent place" in his poetic space-creation, and that although, in *Hyperion's Song of Destiny (Hyperions Schicksallied)* he had apparently once and for all ruled out precisely this kind of permanence: "But it is given to us,/To rest in no place". Never before had the feeling of uprootedness and existential homelessness been described more drastically in German than in the third and last verse of this poem. In it, the time-space of man proves to be a precarious place of residence:

Consequences (I): Measuring Hölderlin's Poetic…

> It fades, it falls
>   The suffering people
>   Blind from
>   One hour to the next,
>   Like water from a cliff
>   Thrown to the cliff,
>
>   Year after year down into the unknown.

("Es schwinden, es fallen / Die leidenden Menschen / Blindlings von einer / Stunde zur andern, / Wie Wasser von Klippe / Zu Klippe geworfen, / Jahr lang ins Ungewisse hinab".)

Time and place are in balance, although the reference to the space, the cliffs, is much more dramatic. In one of his undated letters to his mother after 1806, Hölderlin says that time is "letter-perfect and all-merciful" ("buchstabengenau und allbarmherzig"), a quality he was not prepared to ascribe to space. If one considers that Hölderlin, in the hymn *Patmos,* had described the cultivation of the "fixed letter" ("feste Buchstab") as the decisive task of the poet, then one may recognize a late echo of this statement in the reference to letter-perfect time. The "fixed letter" or the poetic "password" ("Losungszeichen"), as he also called it in *Patmos*, meaning the "rod of song", had now taken the place of the "solid ground", the "permanent place". Hölderlin projected the possibility of being able to continue the work endowed by the poet. The space created by the poem is not "virtual" in our sense of the word; rather, it is concretized in two types of ever-regenerating encounters: the reader/listener encounters the endowed word and, at the same time, in this poetic word space, province and world meet, that is Stuttgart and Athens, Tübingen and Bordeaux, the rivers Neckar and Danube, Rhine and Garonne, thus forming an inner and outer world, as well as merging present experience and the historical world, past and future arrivals.

With Hölderlin, speaking has something decidedly space-generating about it; he does not actually shape his language in form of a sculpture—a task that Rilke was to face under Rodin's influence—but like a landscape. For Hölderlin saw antique sculptures late, probably in the Louvre, but not until mid to late 1802. Afterwards, he reflected on the spatiality of visual art only once, namely in a letter to Leo von Seckendorf dated 12 March 1804, apparently still under the impression of what he had seen in Paris: "The angle inside the work of art and the square outside of it are probably very important." ("Es kommt wohl sehr viel auf den Winkel innerhalb des Kunstwerks und auf das Quadrat außerhalb desselben an.") This means that Hölderlin began to take an interest in the spatial conditions of art and their effect on the viewer, prescribing that he "study them more"; however, this did not come to pass.

Hölderlin's late interest in the structure of sculpture, i.e. the spatial work of art *per se*, remains conspicuous, because it is directly related to his work of translating great tragedies by Sophocles: *Oedipus the Tyrant* and *Antigone*. He seemed to have perceived tragedy and sculpture as equivalents, especially in their spatial design effect. In his "Notes on Antigone", for example, it is striking that he reflects the physical dimension of the tragic action, hinting at the different effects of words on the "more sensual [… or] spiritual body". Hölderlin emphasizes that words can indeed take hold of the body and cause it to perform unheard-of acts.

Hölderlin literally seems to have experienced first-hand what such physical exposure could mean. In Bordeaux, in the southwest of France in the Vendée, he who until then had only made it as far as Hauptwil near St. Gallen and Homburg vor der Höhe, experienced the feeling of having been "beaten" by the elemental, by Apollo himself. This experience shattered him, as he expressed it after his return to Nürtingen, in a letter to Casimir Ulrich Böhlendorff in autumn 1802. His poetic province clearly had expanded. Greece was an integral part of this cultural space from the very beginning, or more precisely: his poetic conception of the Greek cultural sphere, Roman culture in moderation. But, above all, Swabia was part of his poetic province. Now, the strangeness of the French hemisphere as he had experienced it for a few months was added to these "provinces", too: the way to Bordeaux via Strasbourg and Lyon, over the "heights of the Auvergne, in storm and wilderness", and the return via Paris. Before setting off, Hölderlin looked forward to this expansion of his geographical experience with great anticipation, even though he stressed that he would have to "keep his head pretty much together" to be able to stand the sight of Paris, the sea and the "sun of Provence". As a result of this expectation, the world suddenly seemed to be "brighter" than usual, even though he confessed that the idea of not being needed by anyone at home had cost him "bitter tears". In the autumn of 1801, Hölderlin wanted to embrace as much "world" as possible but a year later he knew that he had bought this broadening of his horizon at great expense. Not only had his beloved Susette Gontard died in the meantime. Hölderlin had to reckon with the bitter experience of "foreign lands" unable to offer him a worthwhile alternative to a home which, for its part, did not know what to do with him. Nevertheless, he decided to study the nature of his homeland. What matters to him now, in the autumn of 1802, is to find out what exactly "is sacred to us", to recognize what "the characteristic of the forests", that is primeval nature, consists of, and above all: "[…] that all the sacred places on earth gather around one place" ("[…] daß alle heiligen Orte der Erde zusammen sind um einen Ort"). First Nürtingen becomes for him the place of places, his parlour, into which, according to his mother, he buries himself, in his Sophocles translations, in the great hymns, hymnal sketches and other fragments. In them, Hölderlin actually fulfilled this demand in itself, to group "holy places" around one particular location, for example the hymn *Patmos*, which in a later version reaches out into the Orient, from Canossa to Cana. "… I never knew the lands./But we have suffered much, many times." ("[…] nimmer kannt ich die Länder./Viel aber mitgelitten haben wir, viel Male.") Imaginative empathy as poetic geography: That a poem can become a poetic cultural space, that it becomes a place in itself, so to speak, is demonstrated most impressively by Hölderlin's hymn *Remembrance* (*Andenken*, probably 1803), which, more exclusively than his other hymns, settles in the unknown in order to move from the actually experienced foreignness (Bordeaux) towards the even stranger but purely imagined India—not only for Hölderlin, but also for Herder and, in his wake, for Friedrich Schlegel, the place of culture's origin. This "remembrance" means, first of all, a poetic visualization of what he had previously experienced: Hölderlin takes comfort from memories of the gardens of Bordeaux and the confluence of the Garonne and Dordogne, which resembles to him the sea, over the boring reality of life in Nürtingen. "But it takes/And gives memory to the Sea" ("Es nehmet aber/Und gibt Gedächtnis die See"): The Gironde turns into a medium of forgetting and remembering. The two seem to be in balance. The poetic images also emphasize surprising correspondences: The fig tree in the garden, the elm tree in the countryside, the "defoliated mast" ("entlaubte Mast") on the high seas. The hymn can end with what is probably Hölderlin's most frequently quoted verse: "Was bleibet aber, stiften die Dichter" ("But what is lasting, the poets provide"), because "memory" does just that: It offers a poetic memogram that makes the object and place of remembrance repeatedly experienceable as a lyrical event. The *experience,* in turn, the vividness of the remembering takes place through the respective interpretation of the poem, because despite the unquestionable identity of the place, it retains the ambiguity and thus the need for interpretation. Under this condition, hermeneutics takes on a life-giving meaning: It resembles an interpretative artistic breathing of the poem. For the pneumatic, but also the breath-taking is never far away in Hölderlin's work; already in the first verse it blows in *memory* as a north-easterly wind, which does not stand for the dry-cold, potentially destructive, like the Boreas in its Ode *Vulkan*, but for fresh seafaring towards the southwest. So, in a way he gives breath to the exploration of distances. But what *memory*, like almost all of his poems, wants to create above all is consciousness, reflected perception, mediation between the past and the future. The aim is to create a centre, according to Hölderlin, according to which time can be reversed or "turned back". This, in turn, means that poetry should result in a different, mythologically understood quality of time and culture.

The intensified poetic and real search for a "fixed place" to settle after returning from France happened, on Hölderlin's part, in conjunction with the search for a precise geography for his words, perhaps better termed a logography. In poetic and material terms, this space began with his elegy *Der Gang aufs Land* (*The Walk to the Country*) and stretched as far as his concern for the page layout of his Sophocles translations. In April 1804, Hölderlin wrote to his publisher Wilmans that the "solidity" of the letters, and thus the strength of the word, should remain recognisable even in typography.

However "firm" the printed image of the letters, however "firm" the appearance of the word may be, *the* big question that runs through so many of Hölderlin's poems is: How can the wanderer gain firm ground under his feet? How far beyond the "border of the land" (in the elegy *Stuttgart*) may he venture in order to still be able to hope for a blessed return? In Hölderlin's work, the motifs "Return to the homeland" and "Homecoming" are almost contrapuntal to the path that leads into the distance. On the one hand, the wanderer confesses to having "questioned all the paths of the land" and exhausted the possibilities of home (*Elegy*) and on the other hand, he reaches out into the historical and imaginative space of the Aegean archipelago, where the question of "return" becomes an ornithological one: "Do the cranes return to you, and do the ships again/seek the course to your banks?" ("Kehren die Kraniche wieder zu dir, und suchen zu deinen/Ufern wieder die Schiffe den Lauf?")

Hölderlin's poetic province included his "blissfully Suevien" ("glückselig Suevien"), Switzerland, the Lindau-Como axis, for him the two "gates" on both sides of the Alps, and ever so often Greece. Imagining Suevien acts on him like a kind of ferment, permeates almost every spatial dimension in Hölderlin's poetry; this province, however, also reached as far as the "Caucasus", as it is called in the rhapsodic hymn *Die Wanderung*. It seems that this province was designed for an ever-expanding linguistic area, whereby its most unsteady inhabitant, the poet, admits: "For whatever dwells/Close to its origin is loath to leave the place." ("Schwer verläßt,/Was nahe dem Ursprung wohnet, den Ort.")

Being a poet, however, demands that one detaches oneself from the familiar, even if the surroundings suggest that "there would be/nowhere else to live better" ("es wäre/Sonst nirgend besser zu wohnen") than "on Neckar's pastures, on the Rhine", as Hölderlin's ego is expressed in this poem. Hölderlin's poems oscillate between the depiction of processes of detachment and the longing for return; it is a poetry that seeks to achieve emancipation from the homeland, but which relativizes if not revokes it—often in the same poem.

If one takes a closer look at Hölderlin's poetic province, his cultural area, then one is struck by how emphatically this poet thematized cities, how he made the city motif a constitutive element of his poetry, and this in clear contrast to the German-language poetry of his time. The city, the urban, is almost omnipresent in his hymns and elegies, and by no means only in the form of a clichéd contrast between city and country, whereby the country would have a merely idyllic quality, and the city a merely alienating one. That a city can have a part in the idyllic is proven by the elegy *Stuttgart*. Not Klopstock, nor Schiller would have been prepared to place an entire elegy under the sign of a city. At best we could compare Hölderlin to William Wordsworth here, given his great poem "The Prelude", the fifth part of which places London in the poetic picture, together with his poems "Composed Upon Westminster Bridge" and "London, 1802", one might also evoke William Blake's poem "London".

"Happy Stuttgart, receive the stranger kindly!" ("Glückliches Stuttgart, nimm freundlich den Fremdling mir auf!") The city is seen as a place of integration, whereby the city's happiness lies precisely in the fact that it is large enough, in the sense of being sufficiently broad-minded, to be able to receive, accommodate, and integrate the stranger. City and country opening up to each other—this image appears in Hölderlin's poetry at least as often as the demarcation of the city from the country. It would be absurd to speak of an urbanizing tendency in these poems. Obviously, Hölderlin was not concerned with poetizing the social reality of the city. But he did bring the civilizing fact of "city" into his lyrical consciousness, calling up city names, Rome, Athens of course, but also Avignon, London even, not Paris though, and reflected on their "solid" built existence, only surpassed by the "securely built Alps", as one fragment says.

The ode *Vulkan* (*Volcano*) knows that forces of nature and fate can shake any town planning, as does the "Vatican" fragment that quotes the "destroyed cities". Hölderlin does of course speak of the cities, and thus especially of his "Stuttgart", "Heidelberg", allusions to Tübingen or the Dionysian-looking "wine city" as an advocate of the Greek idea of polis. The polis is for him the model for a community in which balance is possible, individualism and creative togetherness. The urban experience of Hölderlin's protagonist, Hyperion, bore the name Smyrna in Asia Minor, today's Izmir. Although he became disgusted with this city after some time, he was initially attracted by the "sociable city dwellers", as he writes. And he continues: "I enjoyed the absurdity of their customs like a child's farce, and because I was by nature beyond all the established forms and customs, I played with all of them, and put them on and took them off like carnival costumes" ("Der Widersinn in ihren Sitten vergnügte mich, wie eine Kinderposse, und weil ich von Natur hinaus war über all' die eingeführten Formen und Bräuche, spielt' ich mit allen, und legte sie an und zog sie aus, wie Fastnachtskleider."). It has been rightly pointed out that this passage on the criticism of the city corresponds exactly to the attitude of Rousseau in his *Nouvelle Héloïse*, which criticizes civilization and in which it says, with reference to city life, that "everything about it is absurd"; but what seems decisive is that this urban nonsense was able to attract Hyperion and that he learned to play with it, which is by no means the case with Rousseau.

Hölderlin addresses Heidelberg as a mother in his ode of the same name written in the summer of 1800. Since his first visit in June 1788, he regarded Heidelberg as an ideal image of a "rural beauty" with "cheerful alleys" and "fragrant gardens", but above all with a "strange" bridge, which is mentioned twice in the ode. He even speaks of a magic that emanates from this bridge and that has bound the subject of the ode to it. The bridge is the place where country and city meet and merge. It is a *locus transitionis*, place of transition, but *within* the poetic cultural space. The alleys of Heidelberg are also "cheerful" because they benefit from this reciprocal connection between city and country, whereby the equivalent of the bridge is the "fateful castle" in the sense that it represents a transition from the present time of the city to the mythical-historical time. Hölderlin emphasizes that this castle was "torn apart" by the "weather", i.e. by eroding forces of nature, and did not fall victim to historical powers.

The *Archipelagus* provides the exact counter-image to this, the bridgeless city of Mother Athena with "desolate alleys and mourning gardens", the metropolis devastated by history, to which the wanderer cannot avoid returning. Hölderlin's cultural area includes "safe borders", "the mother's house", the possibility of "crossing over and returning", as he says in the *Patmos* hymn. This double movement of transgression and regression did not only occur poetically; it resulted from Hölderlin's life experience. In this poetic cultural area, Hölderlin said the "language of lovers" should be considered the "language of love" as the language of the native land of love. But despite all his "knowledge of fate", a basic condition of enlightened existence should never be disregarded: "Man should test everything [...]/And understand the freedom to set out wherever he wants" ("Alles prüfe der Mensch [...]/Und verstehe die Freiheit,/ Aufzubrechen, wohin er will")—this is the important emancipatory thesis at the end of his ode *Curriculum Vitae,* or "Lebenslauf".

The coordinates in the cultural-poetic space created by Hölderlin's poems are aimed at a focal point to be newly determined from poem to poem, in which the symbols of the cultures meet, as he suggests in his fragment "And to feel with life", in which he calls upon Scotland, Lombardy, and the "Egyptian", who "sits bare-breasted/always singing [...]" ("offnen Busens sitzt/Immer singend"), yet seems, somewhat surprisingly, to be "poignant". This space that conceals focal points is a place of constant surprises, which Hölderlin owes to his strongly associative poetry. It is a space where unexpected relationships can arise, where everything can relate to everything else.

In Hölderlin's poetry experiences such as the salvaged space, and what the *Archipelagus* calls "tearing time", the return to this space and the shock of being torn from time, formed a network of precarious correspondences. This poetry seeks to put a stop to the destabilizing forces in life by opening up supposedly safe spaces. On the other hand, as an extract of a landscape of poetic province, these spaces also offer the possibility of letting the most disparate interact with one another. Hölderlin succeeded in doing this on a grand scale in every respect in his anthem *Friedensfeier* (*Celebration of Peace*). The first verses begin by introducing the space of the poem, the "old-built/hall blessed by having been inhabited" ("altgebauten/Seliggewohnten Saal"), which is on the one hand a resonance room for the "heavenly, silently echoing" sounds, and on the other hand a banqueting hall, decorated with the fruits of the earth and "golden-wreathed chalices". This hall actually offers space for a whole world province; its interior resembles an inward-facing landscape. But this is also true: the more historical-philosophical the dimension, the more the "image of time", which imitates the eternal, unfolds, the larger this hall seems to become. Whatever is possible in this hall in terms of encounters, quarrels, reconciliation, the pleasurable experience of the moment, and the presence of the metaphysical, is to be conditioned, as seen already, by an elementary "law of fate": "That, when silence is broken, there is also a language" ("Daß, wenn die Stille kehrt, auch eine Sprache sei"). It is then the word that matters when the silence turns and the conversation is to begin, determined by the commandment of the "beautifying law" and inspired by Aion, the "silent God of time", whose counterpart, Chronos, is the God of "raging" time. However, for this law to be recognized in its balancing and harmonizing effect by those who have gathered, or will gather, in this hall steeped in history to make peace, both the silent and the raging must be equally present. In this space, in fact, different levels of time interact with one another; so do moods, forms of faith: Christian, pagan, "signs of love", and language marked by silence. Hölderlin does not, however, describe a dialectical process in this way; rather, the hymn ends with a commitment to letting things mature. The "dawn before time […]/ to the light", the immature and the discord that germinates in it, "fearsomely busy" ("furchtsamgeschäftiges"), as the hymn says.

Hölderlin's poetic space, it has already been mentioned, presents itself to us always also as a space of resonances. At first his countless invocations seem to echo in him: "You, cities of the Euphrates!/You, alleys of Palmyra!" ("Ihr Städte des Euphrats!/Ihr Gassen von Palmyra!"), invocations which in their emphasis want to be signals to cross the border of the country. But more concretely, it could be the sound of the "gloriously tuned" organ, which sounds in the "holy hall" of the church as it did at the beginning of the fragmentary hymn *At the Source of the Danube*. Hölderlin's daring analogy proves the synaesthetic trait of his hymnic poetry: he compares the organ's prelude, which fills the sacred space through "inexhaustible tubes", the organ pipes, "swelling in pure", with the source of the Danube, the source of a river that will flow through wide landscapes, even more than the Rhine. The mere mention of the Danube refers to the "East", making the hymnist think of the Kithäron and the rocks of Parnassus, where even the echo of Asia can be heard. Ionia and Arabia can likewise merge into each other under these associative circumstances. This is not only synaesthetically thought and felt; with such hymnic approaches Hölderlin virtually pursued a synthetic topology and imagined geography. Even the most provincial corner, such as "the corner of Hahrdt," could become worldly, because it was touched by fate and history in the form of the expelled Duke Ulrich von Württemberg.

As expansionist as Hölderlin's poetic conception of the world may appear, its core seems to lie in his need to project his introspection, which had something iridescent about it—in the sense of colourfulness, equally oriented to Schiller—even if it was at an increasing distance from him. This poetry was created in a consciously experienced area of tension between cosmopolitanism and the conditions of the province, the will to engage with the wide world and deep sympathy with the world of origin. There was one thing these (in-between) spaces and halls certainly did not know: Indifference. It was alien to Hölderlin, who knew only too well that a God spoke when there was a thunderstorm over these spaces, to him who left no doubt that even the slightest movement, but also the most emphatic utterance, could prove only one thing: Passion for the word.

"Deep down lies/The levelled sea of the world, glowingly" ("Tief aber liegt/Das ebene Weltmeer, glühend"). Such a realisation was finally followed by a walk into self-containedness in the Swabian province on the all too lazy Neckar River in the semi-circular tower room, in the innermost of all rooms for a fate that was slowly burning out.

Consequences (II): Hölderlin and Homeland ("Heimat")

Godwi, the protagonist in Clemens Brentano's 1801 novel of the same title, quotes the following verses: "As wide as the world,/As powerful the mind,/As much strangeness he holds,/So much homeland is his gain." But in the novel Godwi does not quite know what to do with this quotation. Is "world" and "home" a contradiction? As it happened this question was equally relevant to Hölderlin. From an anthropological point of view, Adolf Portmann argued in 1953 that as long as man is the type of person "whom we know as human beings today", he is Ptolemaic, i.e. primarily earth-oriented: "However far thought and fantasy wander, they always initially work with the images of an original experiential bond, to which the earth is a real home". He also refers to Mircea Eliade, who speaks of a "mystical solidarity" with home.

Those who do not have this, those who have been denied this primary sense of home, often remain complete strangers to themselves, not even a guest in their own dark world.

Foreign, more foreign, wildly-foreign: A strange word coinage in German as an expression of the extreme heightening of the unfamiliar: The wildly-foreigner. Woe to him who has no home, as Nietzsche was to say; the uprooted one is considered to be fair game, a poacher in existence. Hölderlin, who made one attempt after another to break away from his homeland, to tear himself away, only to try again and increasingly in vain to gain a new foothold in his homeland, was described by those who knew him as civilized as a savage after his French campaign. Friedrich Wilhelm Schelling, a formerly close friend from their student days in Tübingen, described Hölderlin as such in a letter to Hegel in July 1803: "His appearance was shocking to me: he neglected his outward appearance to the point of disgust and, even though his way of speaking was less indicative of madness, he completely adopted the outward manners of those who were in that state". At this sight, even Schelling lost the desire for philosophical reflections, which he could have engaged in, considering the situation of his student friend. Hölderlin as a more or less noble savage of a Rousseauian denomination? At least Schelling perceives the discrepancy between Hölderlin's outward appearance and what he says and how he says it. Hölderlin may seem absent-minded to him, but he is not mentally savage. Does Hölderlin play the homeless man because he had realized that he could not break away from it in any other way?

Schelling had last heard of his friend from Homburg; that had been in July 1799. There, Hölderlin, sympathetic to the union of science and life, heart and mind, reality and idealism, had wanted to make a home for himself in the form of a new journal, with the remote, not to say wildly strange name "Iduna", the wife of the Nordic god of poetry named Bragis, who guarded the apples of immortality, the consumption of which kept the gods young. Hölderlin had written that the "non-material genius" could "not exist without experience, and the soulless experience could not exist without genius." And now, four years later, he appeared to Schelling as "formless", albeit in a bizarrely soulful way.

Hölderlin wrote to his by now famous friend, Schelling, back in 1799, that he had thought for a long time about education and the educational instinct from which he saw art emerge; in July 1803, this very friend recommended to Hegel, once the third member of the Tübingen League, that he should look for a position as court master for Hölderlin, which would rebuild him as he seemed to be alienated from human society "from the bottom up". Hölderlin was not caught between places but between homelands, the real one in Swabia, the spiritual one in Greece, the one of friends and the mythical one, which lay where "Apollo had beaten him". Where did he himself believe he was? Where "all the sacred places on earth are gathered around one place" ("alle heiligen Orte der Erde zusammen sind um einen Ort"). Where was that? "In coming and going", he wrote to Böhlendorff in the autumn of 1802, in the "woods", in Nürtingen outside his window, which was immersed in "philosophical light" or reflected it.

"The more I study nature in my domestic environment, the more I am taken by it." ("Die heimatliche Natur ergreift mich auch um so mächtiger, je mehr ich sie studiere.") By this Hölderlin probably meant not only his ancestral homeland, but also other homelands, such as those in the Vendée, destroyed by the revolution, or those of the "southern man" who, as Hölderlin saw it, had grown up in the "ruins of the antique spirit". *The domestic environment*—that is nature as homeland and the character of the homeland. The more knowledge (in the sense of knowledge and wisdom of the heart) this homeland refugee and homeland prisoner

Friedrich Hölderlin acquired about the meaning of "homeland", the more ("powerfully") it captivated him. This was not a matter of self-empowerment in the sense of increased subjectivity, but of the very idea of homeland taking possession of him.

> [...] For whatever dwells
> Close to its origin is loath to leave the place.
> And so your children, the towns,
> By the distantly glimmering lake,
> By Neckar's willows, and by the Rhine,
> They all think that
> Nowhere else could be better to live.
>
> But I am Caucasus-bound!

> (Schwer verläßt,
> Was nahe dem Ursprung wohnet, den Ort.
> Und deine Kinder, die Städte,
> Am weithindämmernden See,
> An Neckars Weiden, am Rheine,
> Sie alle meinen, es wäre
> Sonst nirgend besser zu wohnen.
>
> Ich aber will dem Kaukasos zu!)

This passage from Hölderlin's poem *Die Wanderung* (1801) clearly illustrates his problem with the "principle of home". He, the poet whose ego this hymn is dedicated to, is on the one hand searching for the origin of all culture; on the other hand, he understands the homeland (i.e. of every individual) as a symbol of this very origin, where it is supposed to be good to live. To detach oneself from it, the hymn says, is "difficult" precisely because this specific homeland seems to have everything, including the promise of vastness in the form of the "widely dawning" lake.

For Hölderlin, "home" is partly a clearly defined, geographically concrete living space, and partly a spiritual experience. Homeland can thus be the *hen kai pan*, living in the one and all, or the (inevitably paradoxical) remaining at the flowing place, the water, the river, the Neckar, Rhine or Acheron. Home refers to settling down or being settled down. But this is exactly what the I of the hymn wants to tear itself away from. *But I want to go to the Caucasus!* One could not think of a more drastic contrast to the domesticity of a provincial town in Swabia. If one were to recite this passage from the hymn *Die Wanderung*, then it would be quite conceivable to read the previous verses with a slight inflection of dialect, only to switch to *pure* High German at this proclamation, through which this change from the deceptive homeliness of the traditional environment to the boundlessness of being a migrant would express itself. But first of all, the path to myth seems to be mapped out before the wanderer can hope to really reach the Caucasus.

When does one feel the urge to write about "home"? When one grapples with it? When it becomes too close and too intrusive? When one is about to lose it, or after one has actually lost it? It was probably in the summer of 1798 that Hölderlin wrote the poem *The Homeland (Die Heimat)*, in Frankfurt, in the house of the Gontard family, where tensions between him, the tutor, and the master of the house dramatically intensified. "Make do with the little poems," he wrote to a friend, to whom he confessed that only a few people really believed in him and his art. "… the harsh judgments of men will probably haunt me until I am finally gone, at least from Germany." ("… die harten Urteile der Menschen werden wohl so lange mich herumtreiben, bis ich am Ende, wenigstens aus Deutschland, fort bin.")

The Homeland

The boatman returns happily to the calm stream
From distant islands where he harvested;
  I too would like to return home;
    But what have I, like sorrow, reaped? –

You fair shores, you who raised me,
  Do you allay the suffering of love? Ah! hand back,
    To me, you woods of my childhood, should I
      Come to you now, the silence once again?

(Die Heimat

Froh kehrt der Schiffer heim an den stillen Strom
Von fernen Inseln, wo er geerntet hat;
  Wohl möchte' auch ich zur Heimat wieder;
    Aber was hab' ich, wie Leid, geerntet? –

Ihr holden Ufer, die ihr mich auferzogt,
  Stillt ihr der Liebe Leiden? Ach! Gebt ihr mir,
    Ihr Wälder meiner Kindheit, wann ich
      Komme, die Ruhe noch Einmal wieder?)

One "home" at least seemed certain to the poet: that in the word, even if, or precisely because, it was made submissive to the alcaic, a "foreign" meter. This "home" presents itself as a short verse, as if it were the abbreviation of a feeling. Both verses close with a very anxious question. They are questions of a man who wants to return, but, as he fears, empty-handed. His only possession is "love's suffering". This lyric subject envies the "happy boatman", who has made it a habit to return home. The rich harvest is part of his trade, so to speak. It is expected of him, but also of the poet. He must bring in words, one way or another. But not even that can be certain for the poet of this short ode. He wants peace of mind from those banks and forests, which he once left behind. However, this means that he had originally become restless there and fallen into a mood that nurtured his desire to depart. In a second short ode (*Human Applause*) from that time, Hölderlin, fired by his love, called himself "prouder and wilder,/richer in words and emptier" ("stolzer und wilder,/wortereicher und leerer")—not "*but* emptier", notice, but *and*, as if the richness of words and inner emptiness were but the same thing.

Hölderlin's poem is on the verge of idealizing home. Therein lies the second function of both questions. Together with the "foreign" verse metre, they prevent this commitment to homeland from degenerating into kitsch. He who questions does not glorify.

These verses describe one of Hölderlin's basic problems, which will increase almost to the point of immoderation in the following period and lead to one personal ordeal after another: The desire to "break open", driven by the "divine fire", to seek the "open", only to hope again for "homecoming", carried by the "playing of strings". Barely two years after this short verse, the great elegies will be dedicated to this very state of tension. When he then sums up the state of "harvest" in the poem *Half of Life*, the balance is sobering. The homeland then appears "speechless and cold". The "holiness" of the shores, which was mentioned in the ode *Heimat*, has by now shifted to the swans; since Horace, they are the symbol of the divinely inspired poet. Their "home" will be their reflection on the lake into which they "dip their heads".

Such an intense self-reference is not yet found in the ode *Heimat*, even though the ego has already positioned itself centrally in this poem. "Should I rest? Should I compel love,/ Who fierily pursues the ideal of beauty?" ("Ich sollte ruhn? Ich soll die Liebe zwingen,/Die feurigfroh nach hoher Schöne strebt?") Thus, Hölderlin had composed rebellious poems two years earlier—far from all thoughts of homeland.

However, the worsening situation in the house of the Gontards, the poet's love for Susette-Diotima, his mere presence there was in the process of destroying a "home", namely that of the Gontard family. In Frankfurt he became an alien. Thereafter, he could no longer settle anywhere. And when he finally returned to the "holy shores" of his actual home, he was taken for a stranger there as well. Now, the banks of the Neckar and the native forests were to become places of confusion and mental derangement for him.

"Home" that is something that we only seemingly own; it usually appears to us as an alienating "Otherness", even though the homeland, if viewed from a distance, can become an object of longing. Home is the name given to a sphere and sentiment which one cannot come to terms with, but which takes possession of us, and usually when we least expect it.

In terms of miles, it is not far from Frankfurt am Main to Bad Homburg vor der Höhe, and yet, for Hölderlin, there were worlds between these two places, between the house of the banker Gontard in an affluent patrician setting and his new home in the house of the Homburg glazier Wagner in a tiny principality. And so again, a new home was on offer, again the attempt to put down roots. At court Hölderlin is allowed to give the "Torquato Tasso", so to speak. That he was familiar with Goethe's drama at the time can be considered likely. Even a real princess appears in this "play" on the Homburg miniature stage, as it were, although her name was Auguste and not, as in Goethe's drama, Leonore von Este. Antonio Montecatino is played by Sinclair, Hölderlin's new friend and Minister at large for all trades in the principality.

But Hölderlin does not feel like playing. "The poets who only play/they don't know who they and the readers are", he quoted Klopstock in those days.

Hölderlin recommends himself to the princess with his novel, in letter-form, *Hyperion*. He inscribes it with a dedication text that contains a philosophy of culture in a nutshell:

Usually poets have formed themselves at the beginning or end of a world period. With singing, the peoples rise from the heaven of their childhood into the active life, into the land of culture. With singing they return to the original life. Art is the transition from nature to education, and from education to nature.
(Meist haben sich Dichter zu Anfang, oder zu Ende einer Weltperiode gebildet. Mit Gesang steigen die Völker aus dem Himmel ihrer Kindheit ins tätige Leben, ins Land der Kultur. Mit Gesang kehren sie von da zurück ins ursprüngliche Leben. Die Kunst ist der Übergang aus der Natur zur Bildung, und aus der Bildung zur Natur.)

This means that the poet produces the accompanying "music" for the rise and fall of a particular period in history. The last sentence weighs considerably: Art is a transitional phenomenon, but also responsible for shaping the transition from nature to culture and vice versa. This, in turn, means that art is hardly able to offer a real "home" or anchor. As a *transitium*, art intervenes in the process of becoming and passing away; both turn into material for the arts. Art thus denotes a precarious intermediate state and by no means a secure existence. The very fact that art wants, and has to be, interpreted, prevents it from ever being as "calm" and solid as the natural structure, the Alps, which Hölderlin expressly calls "securely built".

"Every day I go out, and always seek something else,/I have long since probed all the paths of the land." ("Täglich geh' ich heraus, und such' ein Anderes immer,/Habe längst sie befragt alle die Pfade des Lands") Thus begins Hölderlin's *Elegy*, which he probably reworked in the summer of 1800 turning it into *Menon's Lament for Diotima (Menons Klagen um Diotima)*, yet without changing the opening lines of the former. This poetic subject knows its homeland inside out. But whether the "paths of the land" have spoken and answered his questions, remains opaque. In the all too familiar domestic surroundings, the poem's protagonist cannot but search for the traces of a counter-world or at least another dimension. The search is meant for the land of love, "where the songs are true, and the times of spring are beautiful for longer" ("wo die Gesänge wahr, und länger die Frühlinge schön sind").

Where is this journey leading to? To a multiple myth and back, one could say: To mythical landscapes, namely, to Thebes, to the Ganges, to the "cities of the Euphrates", to the "alleys of Palmyra", to the "African arid plains". No imaginary path is too remote to escape from home. To be more precise: The poet traces each of these vast spaces in his true home, his own language.

> The northeast is blowing,
> The dearest among the winds
> To me, because he has a fiery spirit.
> And promises a good voyage to the skippers.
> But go now and greet
> The beautiful Garonne,
> And the gardens of Bordeaux
> Where on the sharp shore
> Goes the footbridge and into the stream
> Deep falls the brook, but looking
> Above is a noble couple
> Of oaks and silver poplars;
>
> [...]
>
> But now the men
> left for the Indians
> There on the airy peak
> On grape-covered hills from where
> The Dordogne comes,
> And together with the magnificent
> Garonne, as wide as the sea,
> The current sweeps out. But it is the sea
> That takes and gives remembrance
> And love also fixes keenly the eyes,
> But what is lasting the poets come up with.

(Der Nordost wehet,
Der liebste unter den Winden
Mir, weil er feurigen Geist
Und gute Fahrt verheißet den Schiffern.
Geh aber nun und grüße
Die schöne Garonne,
Und die Gärten von Bordeaux
Dort, wo am scharfen Ufer
Hingehet der Steg und in den Strom
Tief fällt der Bach, darüber aber
Hinschauet ein edel Paar
Von Eichen und Silberpappeln;

[…]

Nun aber sind zu Indiern
Die Männer gegangen,
Dort an der luftigen Spitz'
An Traubenbergen, wo herab
Die Dordogne kommt,
Und zusammen mit der prächt'gen
Garonne meerbreit
Ausgehet der Strom. Es nehmet aber
Und gibt Gedächtnis die See,
Und die Lieb' auch heftet fleißig die Augen,
Was bleibet aber, stiften die Dichter.)

These two verses from the hymn *Remembrance (Andenken)* leave no doubt as to what Hölderlin's most frequently quoted line ("Was bleibet aber, stiften die Dichter" ["But what is lasting the poets come up with", or "create", or indeed "endow"]) is derived from: Namely a geography that has fallen into fantastical flux (and let us be sure of the Greek *graphein* in this word, the drawing or writing of a world, and geós, being earth and thus "home"). The poet *writes* the landscapes, *paints* them linguistically, gives them memorability. This hymn is about extended areas of homeland or zones, which are geographically intimate and entirely concerned with what the poet regards as his own. It reads like an extrapolated version of the previously quoted poem "The Homeland". The boatman has now been transformed into a global figure, whereby the navigable ground, the sea, is declared a place of forgetting and remembering. One gets the impression, however, that this is also more of a *transitium*, a literally flowing transition from abysmal, quasi natural forgetting and memory formation. What the poets "create" here must have connected with the gaze of love in order to be able to exist, "remain" or "last".

This way of poetic "creating" produces something that is by no means identical with "home", but rather represents an intrinsic value, one which lasts and is ideally fed by *everything* that has happened to the poet. Of course, this also includes an examination of the problem of homeland, which Hölderlin repeatedly attempts to take up, above all in his fragmentary drafts. There are countless invocations of homelike rivers and landscapes: "And Stuttgart, where I/should be buried/May lie, there,/Where the street/bends,/around the wine trail,/And the city sound again/Can be found underneath on level green/Silent under the apple trees". ("Und Stuttgart, wo ich/Ein Augenblicklicher begraben/Liegen dürfte, dort,/Wo sich die Straße/Bieget, und/

um die Weinsteig,/Und der Stadt Klang wieder/Sich findet drunten auf ebenem Grün / Stilltönend unter den Apfelbäumen".) Whenever Hölderlin asks himself questions about his homeland, he tries to come to terms with them in one big breath, so to speak, as if he feared that something might push its way in between. What he feels he can say about "home" takes him to the edge of what is still comprehensible. Home is not something we "have", we do not have it at our disposal; rather, we "feel" it, he writes in another fragment.

What he says in this fragment (*The Next Best* [*Das Nächste Beste*]), for which he makes three attempts to finish, is a more geographically precise description: "Namely the mountain/Goes far and stretches, behind Amberg itself and/Franconian Hills. Famous is this one. Not for nothing has someone from the mountains of youth bent the mountain sideways, and directed the mountain/towards the Homeland." ("Nämlich Gebirg/Geht weit und streckt, hinter Amberg sich und/Fränkischen Hügeln. Berühmt ist dieses. Umsonst nicht hat/Seitwärts gebogen Einer von Bergen der Jugend das Gebirg, und gerichtet das Gebirg/Heimatlich.") But the more precisely Hölderlin tries to proceed in his attempts to describe the homeland, the more the linguistic-grammatical units of meaning disintegrate for him. Catchwords remain that are supposed to catch the eye, one could say. He even considers "Ovid's return to Rome" as a theme, once again encircling the suffering theme of home and homeland.

"Thus the poet holds," Hölderlin notes in the context of these titles and keywords. For homeland does not hold meaning; it rather demands that the poet himself holds meaning. In the end, she, the Swabian homeland, which is as indifferent as any other to her offspring that have grown into non-conformity, left the poet, who sought to salvage his foundation(s) stranded, shipwrecked on land. In the ivy-covered tower "of Tübingen's", to quote an idiosyncratic formation of a Hölderlinean genetive, he was allowed to simulate partly wild, partly gentle feelings of home.

The urgency of the debate on "home" was demonstrated by Jacob Grimm's inaugural lecture in Göttingen in 1830, entitled *De Desiderio Patriae,* in which he discussed the term under the categories *securitas, dexteritas* and *language*, meaning basic trust, a legal order of a community as the basis of personal identity (*securitas*), natural contact with familiar people in familiar surroundings (*dexteritas*) and a common language as a communicative reference. If one relates these elements of homeland consciousness to Hölderlin, then they reveal themselves as having ambivalent values: one cannot be sure of *securitas*—precisely why he refers so emphatically to the "securely built Alps"; *dexteritas* in dealing with (familiar) people was increasingly lost to him; and language became a field of experimentation for him, which undoubtedly made conventional communication more difficult. Greece, in turn, became the spiritual home of this Swabian poet, which presupposed alienation from his original environment. Only madness seemed to have enclosed him again; it was the price he had to pay to be able to retreat to his native realm.

Consequence (III): Hölderlin and the Retrospective Visionary

The nature of Hölderlin's verbal images remains incomparable: "Like ivy hangs down/Branchless the rain" ("Wie Efeu nämlich hänget/Astlos der Regen herunter", *Greece*. First approach); stirring up the signs of helplessness: "But oh, where shall I take when/It is winter, the flowers from, and where/The sunshine,/And the shadow of the earth?" ("Weh mir, wo nehm ich, wenn/Es Winter ist, die Blumen, und wo/Den Sonnenschein,/Und Schatten der Erde?")

The analysis of textual variants and text layers, when conducted with due philological meticulousness, provides us with valuable, even indispensable, insights into the structures of meaning in this poetry. We have thus been able to gain insights into the transformation processes to which the poetic material was subjected until the poet was able to grasp it in the valid form of the elegies and hymns. Hölderlin's poetry lives because it continues to amaze those who engage with it. His verses remain an "experience", to use

Wilhelm Dilthey's unjustly belittled category. One reads and hears only the first verse of the ode *Empedocles*, written in 1797:

> Life you seek, seek, and it swells and shines
> A divine fire deep from the earth to you,
> And you, in shuddering desire.
> Throw yourself down in the flames of Etna.

("Das Leben suchst du, suchst, und es quillt und glänzt / Ein göttlich Feuer tief aus der Erde dir, / Und du in schauderndem Verlangen / Wirfst dich hinab, in des Ätna Flammen.")

For Hölderlin's Empedocles, searching and finding means self-destruction in equal measure. Empedocles seeks the "world secret"; he is the Doctor Faustus of the ancient Greeks. But he does not have to associate himself with any Mephistopheles; for in him everything is inherent, moderation and immoderation, critical reason and rapture. He can heal, but he himself suffers from "the sickness unto death" to use Kierkegaard's famous phrase. In the last verse, the lyrical "I" confesses that it wants to follow Empedocles, "if love did not hold me". Since Empedocles does not set an example by his behaviour; he must not hope for allegiance. By following only himself, and loving the four elements—fire, water, air and earth—more than human beings, he has made his loneliness, his isolation, absolute; in this way he seems tragic to us as he originally wanted to be a teacher to human beings.

In three large drafts, Hölderlin tried his hand at a tragedy that was to contain the "shuddering desire" of Empedocles—a counterpart to the "insatiable longing" of Hyperion. And three times he failed with his plan. Was it the nature of the subject matter itself, Empedocles's incongruousness and over-ambitiousness, that would not but lead to a fragment? Or was the other reason the completion of the ode on Empedocles. In this poem, Empedocles had given in to the "shuddering longing" and spent himself: "... if only you had not sacrificed your wealth, O poet, into the fermenting cup." (: "... hättst du/Nur deinen Reichtum nicht, o Dichter/Hin in den gärenden Kelch geopfert.") Was Hölderlin afraid he would exhaust his poetic faculties, as exceptional as they were, in the face of this enormous material?

Anyone who reflects on the "consequences" of Hölderlin's poetic legacy cannot help but notice the peculiar dialectic of the prophetic and the retrospective in this work. As we have seen, the opening of the Archipelagus evokes the power of memory. Yet Hölderlin does not speak of its illusionary, or transfiguring effect, but of the fact that it qualifies the present, puts it in the right relationship to the past and thus helps mankind to set standards: ".... crying and thanking/soften the proud day of triumph in memories!" ("... weinend und dankend/Sänftige sich in Erinnerungen der stolze Triumphtag!") Memory here seems to have a calming effect. Without memory, no culture is possible—as well as no outlook on what is to come.

Hölderlin's poems do not consist of coherent edifices of thought; abstract thought has been a means of design for him alongside the verbal image, rhythm and special word formation. This implies that a thought once expressed can be re-shaped, re-created. Hölderlin also revised the thoughts on the motif of memory, recollection and remembrance that were presented in the *Archipelagus* in his last great hymn *Mnemosyne* (Goddess of Memory, Mother of the Muses). In it, only dying, death itself, can be remembered. Also "Elevtherä, the Mnemosyne city" is deserted. Memory can no longer form anything that is sustainable in the present. Even mourning denies itself to the mourner when he realizes the extent of the destruction of the city. He can no longer "gather his soul". Desperation seizes him. "You, cities of the Euphrates!/"You, alleyways of Palmyra!/… What are you?" ("Ihr Städte des Euphrats!/Ihr Gassen von Palmyra!/ … Was seid ihr?") In view of the destruction of the ruins of Palmyra by the ISIS terrorist groups, one may indeed ask: What are these former alleyways or wynds, now?

Hölderlin's perspective on history had a visionary character. For him, the past was a poetic image that could be transposed into the future by lyrical means. The "backward-looking prophecy" in the sense of Friedrich Schlegel was an event in Hölderlin's poetry, but also the celebration of the present, for example, when he crossed Lake Constance from Rorschach to Lindau: "Now the city is blossoming and brightening/There in the morning it rises, probably from shady Alps/Come guided and now the ship rests in the harbour/… blissful Lindau!/One of the most hospitable gates of the land is this…" ("jetzt blühet und hellt die Stadt/Dort in der Frühe sich auf, wohl her von schattigen Alpen / Kommet geleitet und ruht nun in dem Hafen das Schiff. / … glückseliges Lindau!/Eine der gastlichen Pforten des Landes ist dies …").

He tried to ward off the threat of isolation: "…the emergence of thought in conversation and letter is necessary for artists" ("… das Entstehen des Gedankens im Gespräch und Brief ist Künstlern nötig"), Hölderlin wrote to a friend in the fall of 1802. Looking back and looking forward are also combined in Hölderlin's letters, as are expression of emotion and reflection. Like in his poetry, the past shines out in his letters as a meaning-image, similar to the "thought" itself, which, as the poet put it, belongs "to the sacred image" that we form. The artist's gaze perceives the symbolic. In Bordeaux, he calls his private tutees "living images of hope", trying his hand as a tutor for the last time.

Whatever Hölderlin undertook, he knew he was imbued with the feeling of the sacred, even if he found himself in bizarre circumstances. He described the following scene to his mother: "These last days I have already hiked in a beautiful spring, but shortly before, on the dreaded snow-covered heights of the Auvergne, in storm and wilderness, in freezing cold night and the loaded pistol next to me in the rough bed—there I also prayed a prayer that was the best in my life until now and that I will never forget." ("Diese letzten Tage bin ich schon in einem schönen Frühlinge gewandert, aber kurz zuvor, auf den gefürchteten überschneiten Höhen der Auvergne, in Sturm und Wildnis, in eiskalter Nacht und die geladene Pistole neben mir im rauhen Bette—da hab ich auch ein Gebet gebetet, das bis jetzt das beste war in meinem Leben und das ich nie vergessen werde.") Even prayer proves to be a self-creative achievement in extreme situations; it is thanks to this very creativity, the endurance of, and persistence in this situation that he believes he is now "hardened and consecrated through and through" ("durch und durch gehärtet und geweiht"). A few months later, he was informed of the death of Susette Gontard, shattering news that may have been decisive in accelerating his mental breakdown—regardless of his attempts to toughen himself against all odds.

"Unbound but/Hateful God" ("Ungebundenes aber/ Hasset Gott"), Hölderlin's later poems (second version of the hymn *Der Einzige [The Only One]*, probably from 1803). But this means: He too believes that he is hated by God, since he hardly knows how to "bind" himself together. The late hymns call anxiously for a God who, paradoxically, appears "gracious" precisely when he punishes; and he loves by hating. Compared with his "hate", the "wrath of the world" can only be described as "barren" (in a fragment of a later version of *Patmos*). As an artist, however, Hölderlin can turn to the Son of God, Christ, the mediator between God and Man. In the end Hölderlin believes himself "rich" enough "to form an Image, and similarly/to look at how he was, Christ [himself] ... ("ein Bild zu bilden, und ähnlich/ Zu schaun, wie er gewesen, den Christ ...").

But in these verses a feeling emerged that Hölderlin called "wrath", which will be dealt with later, the crass feeling of a person who—as mentioned—could get into conflict with his own thoughts.

God and the Gods are angry, Christ however is not. Because, according to Hölderlin, Christ founded the pure word, which is ultimately also a benchmark for the poet. Hölderlin thought himself close to this "pure word", at least at times, since he had purified his language through extreme experiences. Without doubt he had been concerned with poetizing the question of God in secularized times. He, who had called Kant the "Moses of our time", was not concerned with proof of God, but with the poetic presentiment of the divine. For him there could be no certainty of faith; "certain" for him was at best the conclusiveness of a metaphor.

"We have in us an archetype of all that is beautiful" ("Wir haben in uns ein Urbild alles Schönen"), Hölderlin noted in June 1798, and it is this "archetype" of being reminded of an inwardly turned Platonism through his poetry that Hölderlin's "presence" creates. Through archetypes, we experience unheard-of contrasts as "thunderstorms" of the spirit. We should recognize his poems as what they were to his contemporaries: tearing tests.

Hölderlin as a Critic of Culture

Time is "accurate to the letter" ("buchstabengenau"). Hölderlin's mother reads this expression from her delusional son in the last undated letter she received before her death on 17 February 1828. In connection with the *Patmos* hymn, the necessity of maintaining the "fixed letter" had already been mentioned. Hölderlin's fidelity to the letter is striking. It means first and foremost the responsibility of the poet, but also the educational mission of the scribe and scholar, to pass on this accuracy in an appropriate manner of expression. Hölderlin's concern for the letter extended to the typeface, layout, and printing. He expressed his satisfaction to his publisher Friedrich Wilmans when he saw the proofs of his translation of the Sophoclesian tragedies: "I believe that with such letters it is more comfortable for the eye to find the meaning, because one is easily tempted to look at the types with all too sharp letters." ("Ich glaube, dass es bei solchen Lettern bequemer für die Augen ist, den Sinn zu finden, da man durch allzuscharfe Lettern leicht versucht wird, bloß auf die Typen zu sehn.") The "meaning" of a text was, in this case, more important to him than the "letter". Through these translations he had wanted to promote a kind of intercultural mediation between Greek and German literature throughout the ages. This was because the state of culture in the German lands gave him reason for concern.

In the aforementioned final letter to his mother, Hölderlin also expressed the request that the "good God" should speak "as I did as a scholar." It is a speech that he had tried to put into practice as a poet and tutor. Through erudition he wanted to curb his displeasure, if not anger, about the (social) conditions and, at the same time, make this profound irritation fruitful.

It is therefore both peculiar and logical that the next essential hint of anger and strife in Hölderlin's work is handed down in a medium that was itself the cause of the poet's growing resentment. It is Henry Gontard's exercise book, into which his tutor Hölderlin entered his so-called *Frankfurt Plan for Empedocles* at the end of August 1797:

Empedocles, through his disposition and thought, was already minded long ago to hate culture, to despise all functional dealings, all interest directed towards different objects, a mortal enemy of all one-sided existence, and was therefore even in really beautiful circumstances unsatisfied, fickle, suffering [...].

(Empedokles, durch sein Gemüth und seine Philosophie schon längst zu Kulturhaß gestimmt, zur Verachtung alles sehr bestimmten Geschäffts, alles nach verschiedenen Gegenständen gerichteten Interesses, ein Todtfeind aller einseitigen Existenz, und deswegen auch in wirklich schönen Verhältnissen unbefriedigt, unstät, leidend [...].)

Loathing of culture or *Kulturhass*—Hölderlin apparently transfers his own situation and emotional state to Empedocles, who, due to a "domestic quarrel" following his "secret inclination", makes the decision to "leave the city and his home and go to a lonely area of the Aetna" ("aus der Stadt und seinem Hauße zu gehen, und sich in eine einsame Gegend des Aetna zu begeben."). The volcano is the opposite of a *locus amoenus*, or idyll; as the site of the eruptive, it becomes the topos of a corresponding state of mind, the basis of "loathing culture", one of Hölderlin's almost oxymoronic composites, whose inner semantic explosive power cannot be defused even by this multi-layered sentence through which this "loathing" is expressed, which fills more than one page. On the contrary, it unfolds, expands, wants to grasp, or at least touch, all areas of Empedocles' life. "Loathing culture" is not a mere "discontentment" in the sense of Freud, but anger at the bourgeois conditions, anger at their conventions and ritualized procedures, which Hölderlin called the "Law of Succession", which denies the tutor and poet the realization of his love for Henry's mother, his Diotima.

Hölderlin's "mortal enemy of all one-sided existence", Empedocles, will in turn seek death on Etna, self-delimitation in nature; as a project, this tragedy remains fragmentary even after three attempts, unfinished because it proved to be unfinishable like Empedocles's own inconclusive project itself. Could it be that at that time Hölderlin's own "loathing of culture" was more or less unconsciously directed at some forms of this culture, such as its highest, according to Hölderlin, tragedy? Perhaps this only became clear to him during his repeated work on *Empedocles*, i.e., on a classical model that he himself had to create, unlike later with his Sophocles translations. Does this "loathing" not in fact also provide a possible explanation for the almost incalculable abundance of fragments, experiments with Hölderlin's traditional patterns of form and discourse that could not (or were not allowed to) come to a conclusion?

This said, in Hölderlin's drafts no one else in Empedocles's entourage shares this kind of anger at culture with him, not even his faithful student Pausanias. He remains alone with this hatred, which does not run dry, but is directed against him. For he who, as the "mortal enemy of all one-sided existence," indulges in this very loathing to the point of living it out as anger against the conditions of so-called civilization, only has destruction in mind. If self-restraint were to succeed in overcoming this attitude, as in the case of Hölderlin's conception of his Empedocles, then it only leads to self-destruction. Tellingly, though, Albert Camus was to choose lines from Hölderlin's Empedocles as a motto for his provocative essay *A Man in Revolt*, or, *The Rebel* (1958). It suggested that anger, or wrath at culture and civilization, could lead to an inner (and outer) rebellion as well as resistance against convention and traditionalism.

By the same token, Hölderlin himself was, at the time of *Empedocles*, still able to channel his own "anger at culture" into distichs, for instance, under the title *Advocatus Diaboli*: "Deep in my heart I hate the train of despots and priests/ But even more the genius, it makes itself in common with them." ("Tief im Herzen Hass ich den Troß der Despoten und Pfaffen/Aber noch mehr das Genie, macht es gemein sich damit.") Or, turned to the aesthetic, on the subject of *descriptive poetry*: "Know! Apollo has become the God of newspaper writers/And his man is he who tells him faithfully the factum." ("Wißt! Apoll ist der Gott der Zeitungsschreiber geworden/Und sein Mann ist, wer ihm treulich das Factum erzählt.") Were these acts of artistic sublimation of his own frustration with contemporary culture?

Through the rhapsodically free expression, the ode form, the epistolary novel (*Hyperion*), Hölderlin initially succeeded in redirecting the "hatred for culture" poetically. But anger at his own life circumstances remains a subliminal phenomenon and stimulant, even if he can say of himself: "I was raised by the melodious sound/Of the whispering grove/And I learned to love/Among the flowers" ("Mich erzog der Wohllaut/Des säuselnden Hains/Und lieben lernt' ich/Unter den Blumen."). Then, in September 1799, he wrote to Schiller that he had (once again) occupied himself with his early work, *The Robbers* and *Fiesco*, works of wrath in other words, emphasizing in particular the "composition of the robbers", representing, to a certain extent, the poetic-aesthetic transformations of the wrath that speaks from these dramas. In the *Robbers,* Hölderlin encountered the correspondence to the loathing of his Empedocles, namely the anger towards nature that Franz von Moor harbors, even if he later—angrily—rejects the anger: "Anger?—this ravenous wolf eats its fill too quickly" ("Zorn?—dieser heißhungrige Wolf frisst sich zu schnell satt"). He transfers the seven deadly sins to seven destructive sensations: Anger, grief, worry, fear, terror, self-condemnation and despair.

In the context of this letter to Schiller, Hölderlin's first version of the asklepiadean ode *Dichtermuth (Poet's Courage)* is to be seen. It says: "[…] The Maenadian round dance/ seizes him, and the stream the head of the torn one/And his playing of strings turns/He fell blamelessly and nobly/ Dying in a noble profession after all." ("[…] Der Mänadische Reigentanz/Ihn ergreift, und der Strom das Haupt des Zerissenen/Und sein Saitenspiel wälzt/Schuldlos fiel er und edel/Starb in edlem Beruf er doch.") Especially in the last phase of his Homburg period, Hölderlin obviously struggled more for inner (and outer) posture. In the Nürtingen version of his *Hyperion,* the conflict between the protagonist and his counterpart, Alabanda, ends almost fatally, which in life finds its equivalent in an incident that Caroline von Woltmann recounts: Hölderlin had witnessed a "violence of sensation that always went to the extreme. Like Alexander the Clitus, he almost killed Baron Sinclair in an argument over dinner."

Anger, which has not yet become a critique of culture and its formations, gains conspicuous prominence as Hölderlin's life problem and poetic motif in 1799. The message of the ode *Die Launischen (Capricious Ones)* expresses this very clearly:

Finally, I'll be at peace when

    Before, angered by a major insult

I had been straying in the field – Your poets, Nature,
    are angry only too gladly! Mourn and cry easily,
        These lucky ones; like children,
            Who their mother holds too tenderly,

They are grumpy and full of imperious obstinacy;
    When walking in silence, it does not take much
        For them, soon again, to go astray; they're tearing
            Themselves out of the track, balking at you.

    (Ruhig siz' ich daselbst, wenn
        Zürnend schwerer Belaidigung

    Ich im Felde geirrt – Zürnen zu gerne doch
        Deine Dichter, Natur! Trauern und weinen leicht,
        Die Beglückten; wie Kinder,
           Die zu zärtlich die Mutter hält,

    Sind sie mürrisch und voll herrischen Eigensinns;
        Wandeln still sie des Wegs, irret Geringes doch
        Bald sie wieder; sie reißen
        Aus dem Gleise sich sträubend dir.)

The poet, who works on the edge of the mortal sin *because* he suffers from excessive maternal attachment and thus hatred of culture, throws himself "angrily" off course; yet, this seems to be part of his nature. It may have brought some ease to Hölderlin's conscience when he came across the following passage in Pindar's third *Pythian Ode*, which he translated in August 1799: "The wrath/But not foolish/

Happens in the sons of Zeus." ("Der Zorn/Aber nicht töricht/Geschieht bei den Söhnen des Zeus.") So, there is also a righteous wrath, which is admittedly of divine origin; but as a poet and priest of language he may also call the temple of Apollo his domicile, thus asserting a relative closeness to the Gods, for whom Hölderlin will be increasingly passionate until the "divine" *manía* really beats him.

In October of that year, he asks: "What if the ancient waters, which/transformed into other wrath/into more terrible ones/came back [...]" ("Wie wenn die alten Wasser, die/in andern Zorn/In schrecklichern verwandelt wieder/ Kämen [...]")—indeed, what then? In the face of such questions, interpretations of the poem can no longer be limited to the thesis that Hölderlin's poems are a mere form of thought; or that in this poetry the pneumatic is realized; or that these poems are mere places of memory.

But Hölderlin also knew this modification of anger at that time, namely in the ode *Song of the Germans (Gesang der Deutschen)*: "Often I am angry to the point of crying, that you always/stupidly deny your own soul" ("Oft zürnt' ich weinend, daß du immer/Blöde die eigene Seele leugnest"). This very "you", to whom this weeping of wrath is directed, is the "sacred heart of the nations", the "fatherland" with its "higher more serious genius". The angered subject of the poem reproaches his country for its self-denial.

The year 1803 became the equivalent of the "year of wrath" 1799, but the main difference between the two years is indicated in the *Patmos hymn*. "The wrath of the world" seems to have been brought into a kind of balance by the dying John of Patmos through his kindness and alleviating words: "For all is good", reads the almost Goethean conclusion. To quote once again from the final letter of the delusional Hölderlin to his mother: time is not only "exact to the letter", but also "all-merciful".

This tendency continues in the fragment *The Titans*, namely in the phrase "In anger he comes up with it." ("Im Zorne kommet er drauf.") This means that anger can now take on a cognitive value. In his *Remarks on Antigone,* Hölderlin also endeavours to grasp anger—now detached from the Christian context of sin—in a different way. In contrast to Sophocles, "Aeschylus and Euripides were more concerned with objectifying suffering and wrath; they were less concerned with the understanding of the human mind than with meandering among the unthinkable" ("Äschylos und Euripides mehr das Leiden und den Zorn, weniger aber des Menschen Verstand, als unter Undenkbarem wandelnd, zu objektiviren"). Hölderlin thus admittedly contradicts his own translation of *Antigone*, in which he offers a whole range of expressions for anger. His Creon speaks of the "judgement of wrath" and of the "desire for wrath"; the choir knows of the "blooming wrath". For Antigone herself, he reserves the composite "wrathful-pity", a kind of correspondence to the "harmonic opposite" that Hölderlin had developed in his essay *The Reason for Empedocles*. Antigone, however, as nobody recognizes more precisely than the choir, embodies an inwardly directed anger: "You have been corrupted/By angry self-recognition." ("Dich hat verderbt/Das zornige Selbsterkennen.") Thus, as in the fragment *The Titans,* the possibility of positive recognition through anger has been turned into its threatening opposite. Recognition that relies on anger can therefore only be of an unstable nature.

Such anger like that of Antigone comes close to inner turmoil. One could, with Jean Bollack, speak of an "involution" here. He explains (although with reference to Paul Celan's work): "Poetry opens up from within and in this way reaches an abstract point where an origin coincides with autonomy".

But even at this point Hölderlin does not stop. In the ode *Chiron*, which he drafted in December 1803, he evokes the theme of wrath in the first stanza: "Where are you, pensive one who must always/Stand aside, at times! Where are you light?/The spirit is awake, but is angry with me, and/ the amazing night always inhibits me." ("Wo bist du, Nachdenkliches, das immer muß/Zur Seite gehen, zu Zeiten! Wo bist du Licht?/Der Geist ist wach, doch zürnet mir und/Hemmt die erstaunende Nacht mich immer.") The night "enraged" by the waking nightmare or an obsession, for instance, potentiates the "pensive", whose mere reflection to which the "light" can be referred; for this light, the illuminating, prudent reflection could dissolve the "wrath" of the night.

A last variation is again found in *The Titans*, also a *Patmos* echo by the mention of Johnannes:

> Born in the womb
> The divine boy and around him
> The friend's son, called Johannes
> By the mute father, the bold
> To him was given
> The power of the tongue,
> To interpret
>
> And the fear of the nations and
> The thunder and
> The rushing waters of the Lord.

(Geboren dir im Schoose
Der göttliche Knabe und um ihn
Der Freundin Sohn, Johannes genannt
Vom stummen Vater, der kühne
Dem war gegeben
Der Zunge Gewalt,
Zu deuten
Und die Furcht der Völker und
Die Donner und
Die stürzenden Wasser des Herrn.)

This "power", perhaps even "violence" of the "tongue" is *also* the wrath, the wrath of words, which now, however, is again understood as one that has to be interpreted first. The "thunder" as well as its effect, the "fear of the nations", belongs to divine wrath. The late work oscillates between the hermeneutical achievement of interpretation and a non-interpreted powerlessness, whereby anger represents the incalculable "balance" in the background (and sometimes in the foreground). The "calculus", which was so important to Hölderlin, fails before the elemental of anger, which "erupts" usually only when the volcano does, and thus again turns "involution" into its opposite.

In the autumn of 1799, Hölderlin resumed work on the *Odes* of Horace, and he considered the following passage as a motto for his *Song of the Germans*: "Vis consili expers mole ruit sua;/Vim temperatam Di quoque provehunt/In majus" (Violence/Power without mental guidance/without insight collapses by its own weight; restrained violence [power that knows its measure] even leads the gods to greater things.) Wrath as elemental force also appears in Hölderlin's great ode, albeit in a changed form, namely in the third verse, which reads:

You land of the high, more serious genius!
    You land of love! Am I already yours,
        Often I am angry that you always
            Foolishly deny your own soul.

(Du Land des hohen ernsteren Genius!
    Du Land der Liebe! bin ich der deine schon,
        Oft zürnt' ich weinend, daß du immer
            Blöde die eigene Seele leugnest.)

Because this "land" is on the verge of self-denial, the poet is as said angry with it, and he regrets, even mourns it, although the half verse "Am I already yours" leaves the question of belonging rather open. Yes, perhaps it is only this angry crying, the wrathful mourning, the sadness over the "foolish", that is shy, fearful, timid behaviour, the lack of [German] self-confidence that makes the poem's subject belong, and this through the sheer intensity of his feelings, his angry pity for this deeply insecure (late-feudalist) society.

Even if Hölderlin was rarely perceived under the sign of anger, but rather far more as a poet of the sublime, a representative anthology of poetic confrontations with this poet after 1945 proves that the anthology's editor, Hiltrud Gnüg, was able to place a chapter under the motto "oft zürnt ich weinend" ("I often get angry when crying"). Admittedly, the poems included in this chapter only conditionally address "angry crying". A line by Ursula Krechel ironically alludes to the German prototype (the German Michel) suggesting that it was him that Hölderlin had in mind when he allowed his Hyperion to attack German mentality rigorously: "Michel, it does not sing when you speak." And Peter Rühmkorf in his "Variation on 'Song of the Germans' by Friedrich Hölderlin" does not even try to get involved with anger or crying. His poem reads more like an ill-tempered, witty stock-taking of the (un-)spiritual situation of the nation. Only Hans Magnus Enzensberger sees himself called upon to articulate traces of anger and bitterness in his sobering hymn "national language": "what do I have here? And what do I have to look for here,/in this bowl of battle, this land of milk and honey,/where things are going up, but not forwards,/where weariness bites the embroidered hunger cloth" and where the "poor rich" and the "rich poor/smash their cinema chairs with enthusiasm."

In the intensity of his anger and disillusionment, Enzensberger's poem comes close to the feelings that motivated Hölderlin's *Hyperion* in his penultimate letter to his friend Bellarmin in his infamous chastisement of the Germans.

Ludwig Uhland and Gustav Schwab must have had certain ulterior motives when they included an epigram by Hölderlin, probably written in 1798, titled *The angry Poet (Der zürnende Dichter)* in their first edition of his poems (1826). It reads:

Fear not the poet when he is nobly angry; his letter
Kills, but the spirit makes ghosts alive.

(Fürchtet den Dichter nicht, wenn er edel zürnet, sein Buchstab
Tötet, aber es macht Geister lebendig der Geist.)

The epigram provides, as it were, the poetic justification for the saying in 2 Corinthians: "For the letter kills, but the spirit gives life", by asserting that the "noble" anger of the poet is the precondition for this tremendous process. Only from the refinement of anger and hatred, into a critical consciousness, can constructive cultural criticism arise. For anger and hate, in themselves, remain unproductive and lead to isolation—as in the case of Hölderlin's *Empedocles*. From himself he demanded "aesthetic power" as a counterweight to these destructive emotions. In the fragmentary so-called *System Programme of German Idealism,* which probably immediately preceded the draft of the *Empedocles* tragedy, there was certainly a culturally critical finding that its authors, Hegel, Schelling and Hölderlin, had in common with Hyperion: Doubt concerning the meaning of the state's presumptive influence. "For every state must treat free men as mechanical wheelwork; and that it should not do; therefore, it should *cease to exist*." ("Denn jeder Staat muß freie Menschen als mechanisches Räderwerk behandeln; und das soll er nicht; also soll er *aufhören*.") This critique of culture was able to define its ideal very precisely: The merging of precarious social conditions into beauty.

"Monotheism of reason and heart, polytheism of imagination and art, this is what we need!" ("Monotheismus der Vernunft und des Herzens, Polytheismus der Einbildungskraft und der Kunst, dies ists, was wir bedürfen!")

Thus, Hölderlin Came Amongst the Biographers and Editors

Biographies about Hölderlin are often not very helpful. Although one knows the stages of his life, comparatively few details are known. The majority of his surviving letters contains mostly abstractions from everyday life. Hardly a word is to be found in them about what he experienced and suffered as a "pupil" in Denkendorf or Maulbronn; there is little tangible information about his student life in Tübingen. There is not a word from him about Frankfurt (only once does he mention this city at all, in the ninth part of his hymn draft *The Next Best*), nothing about everyday life in Homburg vor der Höhe, in Stuttgart, Hauptwil, Bordeaux or Nürtingen. The biographer gets to know the circumstances of his life from the testimonies of others, his friends, his mother. Consequently, biographers rely on suppositions, hints or plausible inventions.

The afterlife of Hölderlin began during his lifetime, but only when his intellectually active life seemed to diminish. "Some are born posthumously," as Nietzsche aptly remarked when he found himself on the threshold of this state. "It has been a long time since I resolved to tell the world something of Hölderlin's past, his present life, or rather half- and shadow life, and especially of the terrible connection with it, and I was asked to do so by friends of his muse from more than one side". Thus begins Wilhelm Waiblinger's work *Friedrich Hölderlin's Life, Poetry and Madness*, which he wrote in the Roman winter of 1827/28. It was published posthumously in 1831, one year after the death of its twenty-six-year-old author. This first biography of Hölderlin by the young poet Waiblinger turned out to be a pathography of a poet, whom he had revered. But Waiblinger's *Hölderlin* offered more, namely keywords for the subsequent discussion of the "Poet in the Tower". But it is striking that Waiblinger did not mythologize the poet, who was marked by delusion. His findings sound emphatically sober. Let us pick out individual observations: "To complete strangers he [Hölderlin] offers absolute senselessness." To Hölderlin's "peculiarities belongs the formation of new words". He "likes to deny." "[...] I have convinced myself that this incessant soliloquy [Hölderlin] is nothing more than a consequence of the unsteadiness of his thinking and the powerlessness to hold on to an object." As a statement on Hölderlin's voice: "One recognized a formerly good tenor." Hölderlin, Waiblinger continues, was "to himself a subject and non-subject, an entire world and an individual, a first and second person". Now, however, his nervous system is "destroyed and beyond cure".

Waiblinger rarely embellishes; central to his account is his interest in reporting, bearing witness to an unheard-of mystery: the poet of *Hyperion* keeps silent about his past in a "flood of half-French". It remained unclear to him, as it did to all the others who, according to Waiblinger, tried their hand at Hölderlin's biography, whether or not the poet had deliberately fled into oblivion. In his daily dealings with the seemingly schizophrenic poet, Waiblinger arrives at the following conclusion: "Hölderlin has become incapable of capturing a thought, of making it clear, of pursuing it, of linking up another thought analogous to it, and thus of connecting the distant in a regular sequence through links in-between". Waiblinger also sought to trace this inability in Hölderlin's late work, and he quotes as proof the beginning of the "Alkaic Ode", which he titles "To Diotima" ("An Diotima"): "If from a distance, since we are divorced,/I am still known to you, the past,/O you partaker of my suffering/Some good can be called your own —". ("Wenn aus der Ferne, da wir geschieden sind,/Ich dir noch kennbar bin, die Vergangenheit,/O du Teilhaber meiner Schmerzen [the original reads: "Leiden!"],/Einiges Gute bezeichnen dir kann—".) As inaccurate as Waiblinger's interpretation is in this case, since this fragmentary ode certainly has a poetic connection, his quotation proves in any case that he had access to Hölderlin's late notes, to which the prose poem "In Lovely Bluishness" ("In lieblicher Bläue") also belonged.

Waiblinger's critical but empathic engagement with Hölderlin occurred almost simultaneously with the publication of the first collection of his poetry, which Ludwig Uhland and Gustav Schwab brought out with Cotta in 1826. The second edition had to wait until 1843, the year of Hölderlin's death; however, it came with a biographical introduction by Gustav Schwab and his son, Christoph Theodor: "Lebensumstände des Dichters. Aus den Mitteilungen seines Bruders und seiner Freunde" ("The Poet's Biographical Circumstances. From the communications of his brother and friends.") With Christoph Theodor Schwab's two-volume edition of *Friedrich Hölderlin's Complete Works,* which appeared in 1846, Hölderlin was integrated into the Romantic canon, even though Schwab's edition contained neither the theoretical treatises nor Hölderlin's translations, and the *Death of Empedocles* was presented in a misleading arrangement of the fragments.

For the time being, though, this was the way that Hölderlin's work and life could be perceived in its context, but also the "crack" in his existence that Waiblinger had already emphasized. In addition, there was a no less important testimony in terms of the history of his influence, which was published during Hölderlin's lifetime: Bettine von Arnim's biographical fiction in letters *Die Günderode* (1840). Bettine shifted the fictional correspondence back to the last two years of her late friend's life from 1804 to 1806, assuming that the poetess Karoline von Günderrode had known Hölderlin, which was indeed probable. It is proven that she was one of the first readers of Hölderlin's *Hyperion*. And in Frankfurt the following spatial constellation developed, in the words of Günderrode's biographer Dagmar von Gersdorff:

Karoline was already living in the Cronstetten-Stift when Hölderlin, tutor at the Gontards' house, frequently visited his philosopher friend Hegel, who had taken up residence at Roßmarkt No. 15 just a few steps away from the monastery in the spring of 1797. Since the park of the monastery was directly adjacent to the Gontard property, she was also able to meet Hölderlin's 'Diotima', Susette Gontard. She would have noticed Hölderlin's hasty departure when the banker, outraged by his wife's love affair, forbade him to leave the house. Rumors of the tutor's illicit relationship with the wife of his employer occupied half of Frankfurt. The love affair could even be found in the novel *Hyperion*.

For Bettine von Arnim these constellations were, in retrospect, unquestionably irresistible. In Karoline's poems she detected a tone similar to Hölderlin's. She believed to hear in them "the tendon of the bow of the poet-god [Hölderlin] clink". "The echo from the barren land in Hölderlin's soul" sounded like her singing: "So let me be born, as the moment has borne me,/In eternal circles the Horae turn,/The stars wander without a steady stand." In the epistolary novel, she invites her friend to visit Hölderlin in Homburg. One cannot deny that Bettine's fiction is worthy of some credit regardless of her at times fanciful and exaggerated approach and style: she was one of the first to appreciate Hölderlin's translations of Sophocles. In Bettine's account, she rejects the idea of linguistic logic as the only yardstick for the success of translations. Rather, she asks whether a poem or translation makes it possible to let one's own soul "resonate".

In so doing, Bettine followed the enthusiasm for Hölderlin that her brother, Clemens Brentano, and her husband, Achim von Arnim, had. Her point of departure was August Wilhelm Schlegel's favourable review in the influential *Jena Literary Journal* of Hölderlin's poems, which had been published in the *Taschenbuch für Frauenzimmer* in the year 1799. Schlegel sensed, mainly in Hölderlin's shorter lyrical works, that its author "carries with him the thought of a poem of greater scope, for which we heartily wish him every external favour, since the previous rehearsals of his poetry and even the uplifting feeling expressed here give reason to hope for a beautiful success."

Carl Conrad Theodor Litzmann (1815–1890) placed the connection between work and life, between edition and biography, as cultivated by Romanticism, at the centre of his edition of Hölderlin's letters of 1890. Litzmann, who also edited works by Emanuel Geibel, embodied as a physician—he was the director of the Kiel Women's Hospital from 1849 to 1885—the type of the loving bourgeois Hölderlin connoisseur who, as in the case of the Schwab *père et fils*, passed on his interest in Hölderlin to his son. In 1896/97 the latter then published *Hölderlin's Collected Poems in Two Volumes* with a biographical introduction.

The young scholar Norbert von Hellingrath, who was close to the circle surrounding the enigmatic German poet Stefan George, then broke with this tradition of a biographically oriented Hölderlin philology in his pioneering historical-critical edition of works, the fourth volume of which was completed shortly before the outbreak of the First World War. It provided access to Hölderlin's late work (1800–1806) and was to make a decisive contribution to Hölderlin's legacy in literary modernity. Even Carl Schmitt, discredited by his juridical justification of totalitarianism and affiliation with Nazism, remembered this Hölderlin phenomenon in his glossary in 1948:

'Youth without Goethe' (Max Kommerell), that was for us since 1910 *in concreto* Youth with Hölderlin, i.e. the transition from optimistic-neutralizing genialism to pessimistic-active-tragic genialism. But it remained within the genial framework, indeed, it still deepened it to infinite depths. Norbert von Hellingrath is more important than Stefan George and Rilke– precisely because he had made Hölderlin's works accessible to his generation.

Hellingrath had "given the work, not the life story, let alone the illness", as he explained in the preface to the fourth volume. One should not look for the "personal fates of the poet" in the work, but should understand that they had become poetry. However, he was to modify this approach decisively in a lecture in 1915 (*Hölderlin's Madness*). Franz Zinkernagel (1878–1935), who himself had worked on the preparations for his Hölderlin edition, had sharply condemned the—as he thought—hasty action of the "very young beginner" Hellingrath. His review in the magazine *Euphorion* (1914) bordered on slander: "There is no greater danger than that the entire Hölderlin research is exposed to ridicule through advertising and lack of criticism." After Hellingrath's death—he fell as a volunteer dispatch runner in December 1916 in the trenches before Verdun—Ludwig von Pigenot and Friedrich Seebaß continued this edition after the First World War.

Hellingrath had written a dissertation on Hölderlin's Pindar translations, but he had also worked on the question of the poet's madness. His lectures *Hölderlin and the Germans* as well as *Hölderlin's Madness,* published by Pigenot with Hugo Bruckmann in Munich, appeared in 1922 in their eleventh edition. The question of whether Hölderlin was subject to progressive schizophrenia remained as rife as it was open. The Swiss psychiatrist Eugen Bleuler had differentiated between "positive" and "negative" schizophrenia back in 1911. He connected its "positive" side with general symptoms of losing touch with reality, which can happen to us all, for instance when we hear voices, see visions, feel persecuted, regard ourselves particularly vulnerable, perhaps in a state between sleeping and waking, dreams and nightmares. The "negative" dimension of schizophrenia is associated with cognitive decline, social withdrawal, apathy and uncontrollable emotions. Hölderlin must clearly have experienced both sides, perhaps at times many of these symptoms at once. The presence of such deliberations in the 1920s was highlighted by a study in which Karl Jaspers examined the psychopathology of Strindberg and Van Gogh with particular reference to Swedenborg and Hölderlin (1922).

No reader of Hölderlin was more removed from discourses on the poet's "madness" than Martin Heidegger, who was to advocate the untainted "purity" of this poetry. But his treatise *Hölderlin and the Nature of Poetry*, which was fundamental to the poetic turn of his own thinking, was still dedicated to the memory of Hellingrath. The name of the publisher, Hugo Bruckmann, is significant because it was in his Munich branch that Rainer Maria Rilke met Norbert von Hellingrath as early as 1910, and thus came into contact with Hölderlin's work.

Klaus Mann was to write in retrospect that the youth at that time mistakenly believed "that they had to die for a Hölderlinian Germany". However, the national-patriotic interpretation of Hölderlin, which Hellingrath expressed above all in his lecture *Hölderlin and the Germans* held in Munich in February 1915, differed considerably from the chauvinistic tone of his time in one point: On the basis of his subtle knowledge and insights into Hölderlin's Pindar translations, he claimed that the German language possessed an intrinsic Greekism that predestined it, before all other European languages, to have a "genuine" access to the world of Sophocles and Pindar. Hellingrath's culturally conditioned patriotic disposition did not, however, cloud his philological conscience, and even if today one reaches for these volumes with their idiosyncratic critical text commentaries, one can hardly deny them recognition. In the lecture in question, Hellingrath did indeed equate "Hölderlin" with "secret Germany", as Klaus Mann remarked:

I call us 'the people of Hölderlin' because it is deep in the German nature that its innermost glowing core can only be found infinitely far beneath the slag crust, which is its surface; but only in a secret Germany could this glowing come to the fore [...] And because Hölderlin is the greatest example of that hidden fire, that secret empire, that silent, unnoticed image of the divine glowing core.

Was it the front experience that changed Hellingrath's view of the connection between life and work? For what he said at the beginning of his lecture *Hölderlin's Madness* resembled a programmatic revision of the principles expressed in the preface to volume four of his edition of the poet's *Complete Works:*

If I want to speak to you of Hölderlin's life, it is no different than when I speak of his work. There's nothing double or separable. His life stands in a single service [...] He holds an office that they [the Gods] have imposed on him, a legation, and that is all, is the entirety: office, legation, message.
Life *and* work are the expression of the form of this message in the fabric of the world into which he entered. Life and work are like the voice and gesture of a speaker: Soon the words seem to tell us more, soon the gesture more, life is completely filled and absorbed by work, and the work is life.

Furthermore, he understands Hölderlin's "madness" as the "secret" of this life and work, which "enigmatically attracts and pushes away as incomprehensible". This confirms the findings of Jochen Schmidt, who has shown how "Hölderlin's madness was an obstacle to the adequate perception of his work" in the 19th century, since "editors had either not accepted a number of late poems at all or only with considerable hesitation", "because they were afraid to grant rank to poems that deviated greatly from the usual poetic normality". Anything that stood in the way of a comprehensive reception of Hölderlin's poems in the 19th century, Schmidt continued, had even promoted their impact at the beginning of the 20th century. Wilhelm Dilthey's essay on Hölderlin from 1905 played a decisive role in this, emphasizing the experiential character of these poems. Hellingrath's edition, and his comments on Hölderlin's madness implemented this approach comprehensively.

Moreover, by reflecting on the delicate question of the poet's madness, Hellingrath surprisingly professed that *narration* is a form of communication, in other words, an almost anti-philological method. In this context, he gave a lot of attention to the account of a French female aristocrat in 1852. It contained reference to her youth in her parents' castle near Blois and her recollection of a confused German, who seemed to have prematurely aged, who was observed in the park and later briefly taken into the house. He had first conversed with the sculptures of Gods in the garden, later with her father: Thus Hölderlin allegedly behaved on his presumed way back from Bordeaux.

The Austrian writer Moritz Hartmann first published this narrative report under the title "Eine Vermutung" in the magazine *Freya* (1861). Immediately after the First World War, Friedrich Seebaß reprinted it in the magazine *Das Reich* (1919). This episode from the history of Hölderlin research is significant because it shows, in an exemplary manner, how closely textual criticism, biographical narrative, and speculation were related.

From Hellingrath's editorial approach, a straight path leads to Friedrich Beissner's eight-volume *Großer Stuttgarter Ausgabe* der *Sämtlichen Werke Hölderlins* (Stuttgart edition of *Hölderlin's Complete Works)* (1943–1985), and this so because for Hellingrath, as well as for Beissner, the subtle knowledge of *Hölderlin's Translations from Greek,* the title of his dissertation published in 1933, had been the starting point of their philological interest. The same applies to Jochen Schmidt's three-volume edition of *Sämtliche Werke und Briefe* (1992-94), the second volume of which—in collaboration with Katharina Grätz—provided a philologically sound edition of *Empedocles* and the most impressive commentary on the translations to date.

But the history of these editions, which in turn deserves a "biography", is a history of ideological trench warfare. For on the "opposite side" is the editorial concept of Dietrich Eberhard Sattler, which relied on a text-genetic processing of the Hölderlin texts, offering facsimile manuscripts and presenting the complete works as *work-in-progress* (1975–2008). Ultimately, the Sattler Edition (and with it the edition of hymnic late poetry by Dietrich Uffhausen) claims that Hölderlin's texts cannot be assumed to be fixable. It emphasizes the processual in his writing. However, this ignores the fact that fair copies, authorized versions and prints of Hölderlin's most important poems (and of course of *Hyperion* as well) are available. Sattler, however, served the interests of post-structuralist text dynamics, which reject any editorial determination as authoritarian paternalism of the reader. Michael Knaupp struck a perfectly feasible middle ground with his edition of *Sämtliche Werke und Briefe* (1992–93); he retained Hölderlin's authentic orthography and included all commentaries in a separate volume, thus creating a practical reading edition that largely satisfied the demands of critical philological presentation. As in the case of Heinrich von Kleist, Georg Büchner and Georg Trakl in particular, the guild of Hölderlin philologists was always quick to equate the favouring of a certain form of edition with "taking sides". One suspects that this threatens to bring the "cultivation of the firm letter" ("Pflege des vesten Buchstabs", Hölderlin) to the point that it is a parody of philological endeavour, whereby the Sattler school of editing assumed that Hölderlin's letters were decidedly "movable". As controversial as Sattler's editorial achievement has remained, there is little doubt that his Frankfurt Hölderlin edition "motivated the discipline of edition studies as a whole to a push for modernization", as Jochen Hieber rightly noted. What is more: Sattler, once the crass outsider among Hölderlin philologists, a self-taught philologist with no university degree and former graphic designer, who allied himself with KD Wolff and his then radically "left-wing" publishing house "Roter Stern" (later Stroemfeld, incidentally named after one of Hölderlin's line of names: "Tende *Strömfeld* Simonetta"), seemed predestined to adopt the outsider and alleged rebel Hölderlin. In retrospect, it is hardly surprising that precisely this form of identifying philology was met with suspicion. However, it is this laborious and correspondingly long episode in the history of the Hölderlin aftermath that shows how essential it is to agree on ways and means to secure this stock of texts.

And the biographers? None of the above-mentioned philologists have attempted to write a biography of Hölderlin. At any rate, it is noticeable that, after Peter Härtling's novel-like offer (1976) and Pierre Bertaux's depiction of Hölderlin's life as a disguised Jacobin (1978), there are no more recent biographies of Hölderlin, apart from Gunter Martens' biographical introduction in the well-known Rowohlt series (2002). This markedly changed with Rüdiger Safranski's biography *Hölderlin. Komm! Ins Offene, Freund!* (2019). The biography's main motif is taken from Hölderlin's shortest elegy, devoted to a state of being "out of town" and meandering in the countryside—into the open spaces of the landscape. Safranski shows how poetry turned into Hölderlin's sustenance and subsistence from early on. One of his most striking points is expressed in a neologism when he calls Hölderlin "revolutionsfromm"—pious and, at once, revolutionary minded.

As much as the comparatively sparse material makes biographical access to Hölderlin difficult on the one hand, on the other hand it tempts us to make inventions, recreations, simply to tell stories. This approach began with Stefan Zweig's biographical narrative "Hölderlin" as the prelude to the collection *Der Kampf mit dem Dämon* (1925) dedicated to Sigmund Freud. For Zweig, these attempts formed a "triad of pictorial endeavour" to which Kleist and Nietzsche belonged, although Hölderlin set the basic tone. If one considers the large editions of this volume—*Der Kampf mit dem Dämon (The Struggle with the Daemon)* was one of Zweig's best-known books for a long time—then one can assume that it was precisely this biographical essay that had a decisive influence on the image of Hölderlin for entire generations of readers. Zweig understood Hyperion's words: "O rain from heaven, O enthusiasm!" ("O Regen vom Himmel, o Begeisterung!") literally, and saw enthusiasm as the key to Hölderlin's work; for "the Gods die when enthusiasm dies". Wilhelm Dilthey's concept of experience resonates with this approach, as does the effort to find an appropriate term to capture the "Hölderlin phenomenon". Zweig interprets the "demonic" that had worked in the poet as a condition of highest possible inspiration, which corresponds to the "upward" movement that dominates Hölderlin's work ("O Melodies Above Me, Infinite Ones,/ To You, To You", "O Melodien über mir, ihr unendlichen,/ Zu euch, zu euch"). In general, Zweig emphasizes the musical dimension in Hölderlin's poems, as he, like Shelley, had sought a world "Where music and moonlight and feeling/Are one".

Zweig's "Hölderlin" was published after the first historical-critical edition of Hellingrath and Seebaß had been accomplished, and when a new historical-critical edition (1914–1926) by Franz Zinkernagel was about to be completed (it was then published without the historical-critical apparatus as a read-only edition). In his remarks on Hölderlin, Zweig was well aware of current trends in research on this poet, and it is not surprising that he also took over the aforementioned appealing episode from Blois "Hölderlin in einem Schlosspark zu einem Irrläufer werden" (Hölderlin in a castle park becoming a stray), which Hellingrath reproduced extensively, admittedly in the form of a question: "Was he that stranger, about whom a woman in Paris decades later told that she saw him enter her park and talk with the marble cold figures of the gods in the most joyful *enthusiasm*?" (Emphasis mine)

Also in Zweig's case—the interest markedly shifted to the "late Hölderlin" in continuation of the aftermath of Volume 4 of the Hellingrath edition. This can be seen, for example, in Eugen Gottlob Winkler's (1912–1936) biographical essay of the same name from 1936, a jewel among writers' texts on Hölderlin. Winkler, who took his own life believing he was being persecuted by Nazi henchmen, singled out, contrapuntally to Zweig's motif of "enthusiasm", the motif of "melancholy" in Hölderlin's works, but also that of coming too late, as exposed in the elegy *Bred and Wine (Brod und Wein)*: "But, my friend! We have come too late. Though the gods are living,/Over our heads they live, up in a different world" ("Freund! Wir kommen zu spät. Zwar leben die Götter,/Aber über dem Haupt droben in anderer Welt").

Efforts to achieve more balanced representations of Hölderlin that took into account all phases of his life and work were underway simultaneously, for example, in the form of the two-volume work by Wilhelm Böhm *Hölderlin* (1928–1930) and, above all, the biography of Wilhelm Michel (1877–1942) *Das Leben Friedrich Hölderlins (The Life of Friedrich Hölderlin)* (1940), which was based on his three studies *Friedrich Hölderlin* (1912), *Hölderlin's Occidental Turn* (1923) and *Hölderlin und der deutsche Geist (Hölderlin and the German Spirit)* (1924). Michel, Büchner Prize winner in 1925, who had already presented one of the first studies on Rainer Maria Rilke twenty years earlier, succeeded with his Hölderlin biography in producing a work that is still readable today and which only rarely compromises with the evil spirit of the time, especially so in the final chapter "Hölderlin and posterity", which identifies Hölderlin far too demonstratively with what is supposed to be the "incarnated idea of Germanism". Incidentally, biographical evidence of a different kind has it that the poet Paul Celan was reading Michel's biography shortly before he took his own life in Paris (in 1970, that is, two-hundred years after Hölderlin's birth).

"—I am not writing a biography", Peter Härtling interjects after he lets his Hölderlin (1976) begin rather conventionally: "Johann Christian Friedrich Hölderlin was born in Lauffen am Neckar on 20 March, 1770—". Härtling's first-person narrator immediately remembers that he wanted to write a "novel". "I might write an approximation. I am writing about someone whom I only know from his poems, letters, prose, and many other testimonies. And of portraits that I try to animate with sentences. He is surely very different in my portrayal."

What follows is an "approach" through questions, but also bold and daring identifications with the narrated life in novel form, that is, through a fictional biographer. It is the time when authors begin to parody the genre of the biography, if one thinks of Wolfgang Hildesheimer's biography of a fictitious person, *Marbot* (1981), for example.

The content of Härtling's novel-like biography of Hölderlin is striking in that it creates a counterbalance to the interest in "late Hölderlin"; for it devotes itself to the poet's beginnings, shapes what can be shaped, above all "childhood and youth", "studies", "court master and philosopher". It includes "interludes" and integrates a total of fourteen "stories" into the course of this life, which focus on the biographical narrator and his relationship to the biographical figure, Hölderlin as the "other". A catalytic function for this grand narrative seemed to have been performed by the Marbach exhibition, with its rich material, organized by Werner Volke on the occasion of Hölderlin's 200th birthday (1970), as well as the *Hölderlin Chronicle in Text and Image* (1970), which was compiled by Adolf Beck and Paul Raabe.

Repeatedly we read in this "novel" of a poet's life: "I start again" or: "I invent figures that have existed. I am writing the screenplay for a costume movie. It has long been familiar to me. After reading his letters and poems, I project my feelings onto his actions." This sounds like "Hölderlin and I", and can be at times irritating. Well, I myself recall my first reading impression of this non-biography, back when I was a student in Tübingen (where else?!), in the spring of 1980. I became increasingly embarrassed reading Härtling's take on Hölderlin. And today when re-reading it? Now I feel embarrassed by my embarrassment at that time. For what is actually wrong with sentences like these, which irritated me so much at the time: "He heard the world differently than I did. It was quieter, had different basic noises." Or: "I know he will meet Louise Nast, his first love, in two weeks." Perhaps Härtling did Hölderlin's afterlife an even greater service than philologists could ever dream of. Moreover: would it not have been more constructive if something similar to the Editorial Institute founded by Christopher Ricks at Boston University had emerged from the all-too often unbearable pettiness among editors of Hölderlin's—and, for that matter, Kleist's, Büchner's, Trakl's and Kafka's works?

But back to the Tübingen spring of 1980, where and when there were other Hölderlin-related revelations being read with increasing "enthusiasm", for instance Pierre Bertaux's *Friedrich Hölderlin. A Biography* (1978). It did not begin with the sentence: "On 20 March, 1770…", but with a bang: "Hölderlin was not mentally ill". There was nothing *narrated* about this biography. Its structure seemed piecemeal. Bertaux (1907–1986), son of the eminent Germanist Félix Bertaux and leading activist in the Resistance, appeared among the biographers as a Jacobin with his study *Hölderlin* and, as a sideline, reformed French German studies significantly through his Institut d'allemand d'Asnières at the Sorbonne Nouvelle in Paris. He could have called his *Hölderlin* a "kind of biography", an arrangement of sources that served his psychography of the poet. This book had something of fresh air and draught. For it contained short chapters such as "The Sketchy", "The Silence", "The Kissed Language" (freely adapted from Bettine von Arnim), "The Conversation". I was particularly taken with the chapter "Composing". Who had recognized before Bertaux that Hölderlin's poetic approach was "related to that of the composer"? Until then only one musician, Karl Michael Komma had published an essay *Hölderlin and Music* in 1953, but it remained without consequences for a long time.

No thesis has stimulated—not to say inflamed—the discussion about Hölderlin as much as Bertaux's assertion that the poet "remained true to his Jacobin sentiments throughout his life" and took refuge in supposed madness to conceal this sentiment. The conscious act of self-concealment after 1806 was proven by Bertaux, among other things, by the fact that the "Hölderlin who had fallen asleep" signed not only with "Scardanelli" but also—in April 1837—with "most subservient Buonarotti", incidentally the name of a radical socialist of Italian origin who was known to the revolutionary Gracchus Babeuf and who had published his two-volume history of the Babeuf conspiracy in London and Brussels in 1828/1830. Now, 1837 was also the year of Buonarotti's death, which suggests that Hölderlin was far better informed about the events of the time than had been assumed up to that point. However, Bertaux may have overlooked Hölderlin's fictionalization of dates at that time; likewise, it cannot be ruled out that Hölderlin could have alluded to Michelangelo Buonarrotti with his fictional name.

It is obvious that the answers to these questions go far beyond biographical interest and have a direct impact on the interpretation of Hölderlin's work. Georg Lukàcs, for example, had already read Hölderlin's *Hyperion* as a novel of the *Citoyen*, a thesis that Bertaux adopted and expanded; after all, he saw in Hölderlin's "entire work a continuous metaphor of the revolution and its problems", and in his Empedocles a social revolutionary. For his political message to the people of the Agrigento was: "[…] reach out your hands/to you again, give the word and share the good,/O then you dear ones share deeds and glory/Like faithful Dioscurians, everyone is/like everyone …" "[…] reicht die Hände/Euch wieder, gebt das Wort und teilt das Gut,/O dann ihr Lieben teilet Tat und Ruhm/Wie treue Dioskuren, jeder sei/Wie alle …"). The "true Hölderlin" seemed unmasked. One—that is, the left-wing student movement—believed to have found an unexpected icon in him.

This excitement has long since subsided and insight has prevailed: No (neo-)socialist state can be established in the name of Hölderlin. The way we deal with him gained in subtlety, and this is also due to the fact that his use of language has increasingly become the focus of attention. As a result, one sees in him less the "poet of poets" than the "poet of poetry", an unrivalled linguistic artist among poetic thinkers. This circumstance may explain why biographies of Hölderlin have become rare. His life seems to have been exhausted, but his work remains inexhaustible.

And yet, it does happen that works on Hölderlin that do not pursue a primary biographical interest can provide impulses for a new evaluation of the poet's life. This is what happened in the study *Hölderlin as a Brain Researcher* (2005) by the neuropsychologist and creativity researcher Detlef B. Linke. The title may be as surprising as the fact that Linke's study was published in the *Bibliothek der Lebenskunst* (*Library of the Art of Life*) of the Suhrkamp Verlag; but it conceals a hint at the (secondary?) intention of the author, namely: to take Hölderlin's "shaping" of his life seriously. According to Linke, Hölderlin had pursued a certain life plan, which included his repeated "reinterpretation" as well as the anticipation of his relationship with Susette Gontard in one of the (all fragmentary) preliminary versions of his *Hyperion* novel, "Hyperion's Youth". Probably written in Jena between March and May 1795, that is half a year before he took up his position as court master at the Gontards' in Frankfurt, it contained the figure of Diotima, a copy of the interpreter of Eros in Plato's *Symposium*. As is well known, Hölderlin was then to transfer it to Susette Gontard, which then led to a complete revision of the novel and restoration of the original letter character. Linke also advises a careful consideration of the factors that are commonly cited as indications of Hölderlin's mental illness or "madness". He points out that the question of the possibility of "voluntary insanity in psychiatry is still unresolved". In addition, he emphasizes that Hölderlin's way of life had almost inevitably resulted in "alienation from life"; this, of course, distinguished him fundamentally from Kleist's fixation on a life plan.

Hölderlin's letter to Schiller on 4 September 1795 contains central statements concerning his self-image that support Linke's approach. "The displeasure with myself and what surrounds me has driven me into abstraction," Hölderlin wrote. What is meant by this? The "idea of an infinite progress of philosophy". But in relation to what? The "unification of subject and object" in the sense of an "infinite convergence" of both. That seems to have been the core of his "life design". However, Hölderlin evidently suspects here that this could be acquired for the price of distancing himself from life, while at the same time indicating how determined he is to live despite all adversities: "I freeze and stare into the winter that surrounds me. As iron as my sky is, so stony am I." Who would not think of the second verse of *Half of Life* and its lines: "Woe is me, where shall I take the flowers when winter comes?/The walls stand/ Speechless and cold,/In the wind/The flags clatter." In this version, he had written his poem eight years after his letter to Schiller—again in the unfamiliar Nürtingen—as one of the "Nachtgesänge" ("Night songs") for an almanac published by Friedrich Wilmans in Frankfurt (the *Pocketbook for the Year 1805,* dedicated to *Love and Friendship*).

For all the supposed remoteness of his life plan—Hölderlin wanted to *be effective*, and never more so than around 1798/99, despite the love affair with Susette Gontard. Those who felt a calling to reach the public with their work at that time tried but one thing: To found a magazine. *Iduna* was to be its name, the magazine for which

Hölderlin tried to win the Stuttgart publisher Steinkopf. This plan is only worth mentioning here—it fell through in the spring of 1800—because Hölderlin invited his friend Schelling, among others, to collaborate with him on this project and in so doing overcome his isolated, if not solipsistic, existence. What interested him was the connection between art and the "educational instinct", in particular poetry as a "living art", as it is "at once born of genius and experience and reflection". He wanted to promote this very connection through his journal—as well as through his work in general—under the "aspect of humanity".

Hölderlin gave priority to poetic thinking over analytical philosophy, since in him the "aesthetic sense" was articulated and realized, as stated already in the draft of a *System[atic] Programme of German Idealism* of 1795/96, which had been created through the collaboration of Hölderlin, Schelling and Hegel. For it was under this sign that Hölderlin had also set out to be a poet of thought and a thinker of poetry, who tried to approach the trade secrets of poetic creation and decipher its signs. It is therefore hardly surprising to find Hölderlin's later impact on philosophical discourses—admittedly of a rather special kind.

Existence and Parataxis: Hölderlin's Controversial Thinking—Adorno *Versus* Heidegger

In Hölderlin's work, the problem of the relationship between poetry and thought is exemplary. Poetological questions become verbally concrete in his poems; at the same time, these poems give the impression that in re-reading—or better still: in repeated recitation—poetic thinking becomes evidence. What is continually happening anew in these poems could best be described as poetosophy. What is meant by this concept?

As a "poetics of thought", poetosophy aims at an aesthetic sensitization of the philosophical, as well as at penetrating the poetic intellectually. In Hölderlin's work, this happens with an intensity that could at best be compared to that of Shelley and Keats. Added to this is his experimental character, which distinguishes him fundamentally from Schiller's philosophical poems.

To think poetically means to grant metaphors their own logic, to understand the formation of metaphors as a spiritual-sensual event and, at the same time, to critically grasp the structure of the metaphor. Poetic thinking as thinking by means other than cognitivity, inquires into the truth content of metaphors and determines the effect of their own movement in linguistic execution or realization. In poetic thinking, the forms are activated and contribute to reflection. Their "arrangement and succession" determines the effect of this thinking, "especially in the caesuras, the interruptions in the flow of ideas" (Rainer Nägele).

For Hölderlin, metaphors as images of thought became "watchwords", as it is said in *Patmos*. Both seemingly tangible and practically intangible, they open up paths of thinking towards an aesthetic mode. "And there deep/in the mountains also living images are turning green"—to be seen when one sets out on these paths of thought. In Hölderlin's work, this thinking is expressed poetically, mostly in the form of questions or questioning exclamations ("Light of love! Do you also shine on the dead, you golden one!" ("Licht der Liebe! Scheinest du denn auch Toten, du goldnes!"), poetically in hypotactic-labyrinthine attempts to deal with the "lawful calculation […] through which the beautiful is produced" ("gesetzliche Kalkul […], wodurch das Schöne hervorgebracht wird."). In general, in Hölderlin's constant questioning, this exclamatory aspect may be considered a special feature of German poetry. Yet, this questioning never led to an actual revolt in Hölderlin's work, and if it did, then at best to a sublimated or inward-looking revolt (against himself). Albert Camus states that every revolt is an expression of a "longing for innocence" and "a call to be". Both were also alive in Hölderlin, but without any visible sign of concrete revolt, unless one wants to bring the pathos of Empedoclean anger—as seen—into this context.

It is not surprising, then, that philosophers picked up Hölderlin's poetic model(s) of thought and reinterpreted them in their own sense. The most prominent, and at the same time most controversial, example was provided by Martin Heidegger. For him, Hölderlin became an iridescent field in, and through, which he tried to compensate for his deluded, if not criminal employment of thought in 1933/34. He understood Hölderlin's poetry as an evasive terrain or even a retreat after the tragically failed mobilization of thought for the cause of the Fascist "uprising", which began as a descent into barbarism. After all, "nothing is more monstrous than man", to quote Hölderlin's rendering of a famous choral pronouncement in Sophocles's *Antigone*.

Heidegger's lectures on the elegy *Germania* which occurred between 1934/35 and 1943, as well as on the hymns *The Rhine* and *The Ister* (meaning the Danube), further treatises and lectures, summarized under the title *Elucidations of Hölderlin's Poetry*, revolved around the poem as a conversation of language with itself, the problem of the "unheard-of" or unfathomable, the main geopoetic motif of streams in this poetry, and the question of its "essence". Hölderlin's *Hyperion* with its so-called German scolding ("[…] I can think of no other people more torn apart than the Germans. You see craftsmen, but not people, thinkers, but not people, priests, but not people […]" ("[…] ich kann kein Volk mir denken, das zerrißner wäre, wie die Deutschen. Handwerker siehst du, aber keine Menschen, Denker, aber keine Menschen, Priester, aber keine Menschen […]") is not mentioned by Heidegger. What he did succeed in, however, was to keep the interpretation of this poetry free of Nazi jargon by replacing it with his very own. It is at best described as a highly idiosyncratic phraseology that turned individual concepts into aspects of Being generating out of self-contained philosophical autonomy. Heidegger attempted to demonstrate how this treatment of language took root in Hölderlin's poetry and usage of words, in which he detected the verbal enactment of being. This he identified as a process through which Being and Becoming entered a poetic condition of close proximity. Hence, Heidegger's interest in singling out the liquid medium of rivers in Hölderlin's work, through which the basic phrase "Alles Fließend" (all flowing) gained a new significance.

From Heidegger's point of view, [Hölderlin's] poetry is a "worthy foundation of being", strengthened by the "signs" of the Gods, which this poet was able to capture and interpret. To write poetry in "meagre times" ("dürftiger Zeit")—for Heidegger this included thinking about the trace of the Gods. Arguably, this part of Heidegger's interpretation was consistent with Hölderlin's intention since he had indeed considered his time to be "meagre", devoid of meaning, the poet's word as a foundation "in need". The poet's question, "Why poets [...]"? corresponded with the basic feeling that introduced his "late period" and that lends this attempt its title: the time- and self-critical insight into one's own superfluity: *But they have no use for me*. Yet, Heidegger had suppressed this premise in his interpretation.

Walter Muschg had not unjustly accused Heidegger of elevating Hölderlin "to a salvific seer and bringer of light" and of claiming to "uncover a sole blissful truth about him that had escaped the literary scholars, who had been struck blind." In contrast, Heidegger correctly recognized that Hölderlin was one of the first to make fruitful the symbiosis of thought and poetry, reflection of aesthetic principles and their application in his work. It is consequential that "literary scholars" coming from philology might recognize their own philosophical ambitions and philosophers recognize their respective philological-poetological basis when they deal with Hölderlin—or should one say, work on him. What is inevitably missed out in both instances, however, is the sheer enjoyment that this poetry allows for, the experience of the beauties of the German language, which are founded in the sounding out of its syntactic-rhythmic possibilities and in composing with its verbal sounds, as quoted above, the tracing of the "lawful calculation, [...]" through which the beautiful, in Hölderlin's case, can be produced.

Paradoxically, Heidegger had ignored the historical circumstances of the word-based "Being" of Hölderlin's poetry. Likewise, Heidegger pretended to be oblivious to the historical backdrop of his own engagement with Hölderlin. His concern with this poetry could therefore have been placed under the title: "Being Without Time". Theodor W. Adorno responded to this problematic phenomenon in 1963/64, with his essay dedicated to Peter Szondi, "Zur späten Lyrik Hölderlins" ("On Hölderlin's Late Poetry"), published under the syntactic classification of *Parataxis*. In doing so, he suggested that—as the late Gottfried Benn put it—"everything" is indeed a question of syntax and its art.

Adorno was interested in the phenomenon of sequencing in the work of the late Hölderlin, which he not only compared with Beethoven's late work, but also saw as a sign of the modernity of this poetry, which anticipates future trends. It is revealing, even surprising, where Adorno, the dialectical enlightener of the Enlightenment, sees the point of departure for philosophical discourse in Hölderlin's work: "The darkness of the poems, not what is thought in them, compels us to philosophy." This "darkness" is understood as partisanship for the myth. The myth in turn sees itself as "endowed" by what Walter Benjamin, before Heidegger, had already called "the poetically pre-created", or "the poetic" as such, in his early radical interpretations of

Two Poems by Friedrich Hölderlin. Poet's Courage (Dichtermut)—Timidity (Blödigkeit) from 1915. Adorno's reference proves how important this discussion, located at the borderline between philology and philosophy, is for Hölderlin's aftermath. Benjamin defined the poetic as the "prerequisite of the poem" and as a relational space of, or between, "work of art and life", an interface of tradition(s) and experiences. In the poem, linguistic substance, poetic form and mythological substances—Benjamin calls them "mythical connections"—are combined, whereby this connection experiences its respective realization in the poem. At first glance, this approach is confusing in that—following the common sense of the word—the poetic would be seen as the result of the actual poems. But with Benjamin it is just the other way round: the poem emerges from the poetic as its precondition.

The poem also includes thought. Referring to Benjamin, Adorno accused Heidegger of "neutralizing" the tension in Hölderlin's poems with reality and interpreting his work as "agreement with fate". In addition, he argued that Heidegger had exaggerated the ontological status of what Hölderlin had "thought", "instead of making out its significance in thought". Moreover, Heidegger had largely suppressed the meaning of form in Hölderlin's poem and had not recognized its intrinsic value, indeed, the fact that form becomes active itself, for example in the odes and hymns, which Adorno called the "agent" of such "activity".

What is intriguing about this controversy is that it reflects and furthers the basic relationship between poetry and thought, to which the starting point of Hölderlin's work essentially belongs. Its initial place was the well-reputed Tübingen Stift, or seminary, and later—around 1795—the discourses in Jena, this hotbed of German revolutionaries, that is "Romantic" thought, which was influenced by Schiller, Niethammer, Reinhold and above all Fichte. The embodiment of this intellectual initiation was the early Tübingen triad: Hegel, Hölderlin and Schelling, who, in fact, shared a room until 1793. The fragment *Urtheil und Seyn (Judgement and Being*, probably written in spring 1795) by Hölderlin and the collective achievement of this triad, the "draft" or *Das älteste Systemprogramm des deutschen Idealismus (The Oldest System-Programme of German Idealism)* (written 1796/97), has been identified as the most important document of this interaction. The latter is the later added title of a fragment on aesthetics and mythology handed down in Hegel's manuscript that propagates not only the "end of the state" but the establishing of a "monotheism of Reason and Sentiment and a polytheism of [creative] Imagination and the Arts". Irony has it that a "programme", which promised to unfold a "system" only exists as a fragment, either suggesting that any "system" cannot be but fragmentary or that, by default, the fragmentary has turned into a programme of sorts. Hölderlin could have subscribed to that, but not his friends, Hegel and Schelling; they would have regarded this proposition as a gauntlet. And during the next decades or so, they were to engage in developing coherent systems of thought that appeared to be anything but fragmentary.

In his magisterial study that re-shaped our comprehension of Hölderlin's world and mode of thought, *The Reason in Consciousness. Studies on Hölderlin's Thinking (1794–1795),* published in 1992, Dieter Henrich demonstrated how intensively Hölderlin was able to work through just two sides of philosophical reflection. By means of extrapolations, Henrich attempts constructions that make Hölderlin almost the author of unwritten, major philosophical works. Similarly, Henrich discusses Hölderlin's intended *New Letters on Aesthetic Education,* in continuation of Schiller's intended *New Letters,* as if it were a present work. In fact, one could argue with reasonable justification that Hölderlin accomplished just that, except in the narrative form of his *Hyperion*. Henrich continues to speculate where and why Hölderlin felt compelled to break off his attempt to create a coherent ontology, allegedly because certain thoughts became too "dangerous" for him, a phenomenon at time to be found in the poet's letters, too. From *Judgement and Being* Henrich takes the formula: "Form of knowing self-relation". In Hölderlin's fragment, this relationship reads as follows: "But how is self-awareness possible? By opposing myself, by separating myself from myself, but recognizing myself as the same in the opposite notwithstanding this separation." ("Wie aber ist Selbstbewußtsein möglich? Dadurch daß ich mich mir selbst entgegensetze, mich von mir selbst trenne, aber ungeachtet dieser Trennung mich im entgegengesetzten als dasselbe erkenne.")

Hölderlin reflected on the connection between "judgement" and "being", or more precisely: their constellation(s), based on his in-depth studies of Kant, Plato and Friedrich Heinrich Jacobi's letters on Spinoza. His basic insight quite rightly moved Henrich to place the fragment, *Judgement and Being,* at the centre of his investigations into Hölderlin's thinking.

Henrich's sympathetic thinking in "constellations" can effectively illuminate Hölderlin's attempt to open up "thinking spaces" for himself—initially in Fichte's shadow—from various perspectives, and this is meritorious in itself. As for the aforementioned *Oldest System Programme of German Idealism*, it is striking that it makes use of a self-conscious ego that has become "knowing" through the separation from itself and setting oneself against oneself in an almost counterpunctual fashion. It has internalized the judgement of subject and object and can thus "purify" itself to the primacy of the aesthetic and especially the mythological-poetic.

There is little doubt, though, that Hölderlin's philosophical fragments tempt us to over-interpret—because of the peculiar way these fragments descended upon us. For instance, the *System Fragment* was purchased at an auction by the Royal Library in Berlin in 1913 and edited four years later by Franz Rosenzweig. *Judgement and Being* turned up in 1930, and was only published by Friedrich Beißner in 1961. Since then, the controversies and literature surrounding these pieces of writing have mainly revolved around their significance to Friedrich Schlegel's call for a "new mythology" and thus the connection between idealism and romanticism; it ranges from Karl Heinz Bohrer to Manfred Frank and Rüdiger Safranski, but goes back to Walter Benjamin and Johannes Hoffmeister, who, in 1931 intensively studied the interaction between Hölderlin and Hegel. These endeavours testify to one of the main theses in the *System Programme*: "The philosophy of mind is an aesthetic philosophy". This demand was then fulfilled by Hegel's *Phenomenology of the Mind*; a systematic philosophical novel of education whose protagonist is the mind.

"A Sign We Are, Without Interpretation": An Afterlife in Literary Interpretations

Who would want to deny the connection between editorial-philological achievement, hermeneutic interpretation, philosophical penetration and the extraction of literary theory from poetic texts? There can be no doubt that this connection has been conditioned by ideological guidelines and corresponding expectations for a fair amount of time. Hölderlin's academic aftermath consists largely of experiments of this kind, with the net result that his works belong to the best-edited volumes in the German language.

It would be misguided, even absurd, to demand that Hölderlin be freed from this "ballast" in order to let the poems themselves speak again. For this scholarly "ballast" now belongs to this work, which is so richly ambiguous. But this cannot mean that we should "recite" the commentaries to poems in the manner of how we "perform" *Half of Life*, *Celebration of Peace*, *Bread and Wine*, *The Rhine* or *Patmos*.

This said, all interpretation of these poems ultimately fails if it overlooks a certain precept—not an ideological but an existential one. Hölderlin pronounced this in the second version of his hymn *Mnemosyne*; it should be read before every work about this poet: "A sign we are, uninterpreted,/ Painless are we and have almost/Lost our language in a foreign land" ("Ein Zeichen sind wir, deutungslos,/Schmerzlos sind wir und haben fast/Die Sprache in der Fremde verloren."). Corresponding to this are the lines from *Half of Life:* "The walls stand/Speechless and cold, in the wind/The flags clink." ("Die Mauern stehn/Sprachlos und kalt, im Winde/Klirren die Fahnen.") And when the *Celebration of Peace* conjures up a "law of fate" ("Schicksalgesetz") according to which a—new—language can emerge, "when silence returns" (in the open sense of: Returns, reverses, returns), then this turn of phrase also belongs to the caveats which every interpretation of this poet should take into account. As much as language seems to celebrate itself in these poems, it also shows us its limits, its need to break off before the numinous.

Literary studies search for influences, historical layers of meaning combined with zeitgeist moods that a text has absorbed; they ask about hyper- and sub-texts together with parataxis, or more fashionably speaking: Intertextualities, to use Julia Kristeva's ever popular phrase coined back in 1967. But they still have little insight into the way these "influences" are transformed, which is the main thing that really matters given its effectiveness in aesthetic terms. It could also benefit from increased research into constellations, from investigations into mutual dependencies of meaning and from sounding out poetic periods of thought in which "works" are created and which they themselves represent.

As mentioned before, Hölderlin questioned his own "usefulness" but it appears that literary studies at least "needed" him, if only to demonstrate their unquestionably impressive capacity. Admittedly, his poems set limits to the often bewildering methodologies of literary criticism. Not that this poetry was in any way method-resistant. But, for instance, postcolonially motivated literary research can only add a limited amount to our understanding of this poet. Yet, (post-) structuralists and deconstructivists seem to have (had) their field days with Hölderlin. And with reference to Michel Foucault, interest in Hölderlin's "madness" blossomed anew. The gruesome, albeit for the time characteristic, procedures in the Autenrieth Clinic in Tübingen became at times more important an object of investigation than the poetic work itself, as did the fact that Hölderlin was able to write poetry at all again in his state of delusion or derangement.

Adorno understood Hölderlin's poetry as partly sinister when he referred to what he bizarrely called "a horrendous line", namely the verse: "But I want to go to the Caucasus", as it gave an idea of "what the German ideology would one day use it for" as if it had condoned, in anticipation, German expansionism in the early 1940s. They catch the eye, these references, to "Asia's Gates" or the "African arid/plain", the Oriental and Transoceanic as poetic places of longing and projection (Kocziszky). However, research has not yet been able to convincingly demonstrate any quasi-colonizing intention on Hölderlin's part. This said, Hölderlin did indeed sketch out approaches to a Columbus hymn, which, right at the beginning, immediately identifies the poetic ego with "Columbus": "Do I wish I were one of the heroes/ […] So it would be a naval hero." ("Wünscht' ich der Helden einer zu sein/[…] So wär' es ein Seeheld."). But this sympathy was obviously for the discoverer, not the conqueror, although Hölderlin's use of this term was certainly subject to change. But this one example illustrates just how controversial the views on Hölderlin's use of the word have *remained*. The word "conquer" first appears in his short poem *To Our Great Poet (An unsre großen Dichter*, 1798):

The banks of the Ganges heard the gods of joy
   Triumph, as all-conquering from the Indus
     The young Bacchus came, with blessed
        Wine from sleep waking the peoples.

Oh wake up, you poets! Wake them from their slumber too,
  Those who are asleep now, give the laws, give
    Our lives. Be victorious, heroes! Only with you
      Is the right of conquest, like with Bacchus.

    (Des Ganges Ufer hörten des Freudengotts
      Triumph, als allerobernd vom Indus her
        Der junge Bacchus kam, mit heilgem
           Weine vom Schlafe die Völker weckend.

    O weckt, ich Dichter! Weckt sie vom Schlummer auch,
      Die jetzt noch schlafen, gebt die Gesetze, gebt
        Uns Leben, sieht, Heroen! Ihr nur
           Habt der Eroberung Recht, wie Bacchus.)

According to mythology, Bacchus came from India and from there he "conquered" the Occident with his "holy wine". Of course, this is a "conquest" by intoxicatingly poetic means, whereby the "wine" is paradoxically supposed to "wake up" the people. One has interpreted these verses politically and questioned whether Hölderlin could have meant the transformation of the revolutionary wars into campaigns of conquest (Müller-Seidel); others have referred the "all-conquering" to Alexander the Great (Schmidt) or have connected conquest with the "threatening" nature of wine, but above all with taking possession of language as a poetological phenomenon (Pott). The elaborated version of this ode *Dichterberuf* (1800/01) now assigns the poet as "angel" and "master" of "conquest right". This, in turn, was interpreted as a religious turn (Müller-Seidel), whereby all three interpretations disregard the one-strophic sketch that calls Bacchus the "friendliest of all conquerors", and thus indicates a qualification of conquerors. Yet, there is another layer of meaning to be considered, which may have been even closer to the poet's heart and mind given his religious upbringing. Christ is often thought of as a "conqueror" over sin, death and the evil spirit, as well as a reconciler as a result of this "conquest", so in *Colossians* (2:15).

There are always those great moments in Hölderlin's research that come about when philological expertise, a sense of context and poetological references come together. This can result in works such as Jochen Schmidt's study *Hölderlin's Historical-Philosophical Hymns "Friedensfeier"(Celebration of Peace)—"Der Einzige" (The Only One)—"Patmos"* (1990), Margarethe Wegenast's investigation *Hölderlin's Spinoza Reception and its Significance for the Conception of "Hyperion"*, and Sabine Doering's analysis *Aber was ist diß? Forms and Function of the Question in Hölderlin's Poetic Work* (1992). They stand for a handling of the source material that is as penetrating as it is striking, from which they derive guiding questions that in turn structure their prudent mode of representation. They avoid the extravagant thesis and instead rely on solid argumentation.

If one asks, however, for an exemplary, even fundamental controversy about Hölderlin, which was more oriented towards content than the purely editorial, then it can be found in the debate about Wolfgang Lange's thesis of this poet's so-called "madness project". The debate occurred in 1989, in the renowned *Deutsche Vierteljahresschrift für Literaturwissenschaft und Geistesgeschichte* between Wolfgang Lange and Jochen Schmidt. It simply does not seem possible to get away from the ever-tantalizing problem of Hölderlin's madness and its meaning. Lange claimed that Hölderlin had asked himself the question "how", under the conditions of a disenchanted, highly rationalized culture such as the modern one, a poetry can be created that is equal to that of the Greeks, a poetry in which "fire from heaven" or "holy madness" can appear in a new way. From this, Lange came to the conclusion that Hölderlin had consciously integrated Plato's *manía* into his poetry after 1800. As a poet, he understood himself as a "mediator between the drifting apart spheres of science and morality, theory and practice, the divine and the human", whereby this put him to a constant test. This also explains the "schizophrenic tragedy of his songs", which in another context was also called Hölderlin's "schizopoetics" (Simon Thomas). Moreover, it has long been argued that Hölderlin's idea of the poet corresponded to a way of becoming that resulted "from an erotic affinity between man and nature", "in an act of love [...] in which the sensual and the spiritual merge with one another as in a divine play, in order to rise ecstatically to song out of and in the embrace". The core problem, however, is not even this emphatically erotic relationship of the poet to nature, but rather the "transformation of melancholy into the "everlasting creative" mania, into the madness with which not only Hölderlin struggled throughout his life, but from which, in different ways, the radical-aesthetic-nihilistic poetry of modernity will also take its starting point." That much of Lange.

Jochen Schmidt countered vehemently and with exemplary philological-hermeneutic precision arguing his case thus: "Hölderlin did not want madness, he had no "madness project", rather he worked against madness because he felt threatened by it." Accordingly, Schmidt worked out Hölderlin's poetic attempts at self-stabilization, not rejecting in any way Lange's concern to detect "romantic" tendencies in this work, but calling for a more thorough investigation. While Lange emphasized the poet's erotic relationship to nature, Schmidt pointed out that Hölderlin attempted to resist the distance of "art" from nature, "[…] for since his encounter with Fichte's philosophy he had fought against the ego, which had been made absolute by Fichte, and the spirit, which had become autocratic, as a 'danger'". According to Schmidt, Hölderlin had seen "in this a hybrid detachment from the natural contexts of the justification of existence, which are also those of artistic creation".

Once again, the lyrical linchpin of this discussion proved to be the poem *Half of Life*, which Hölderlin had peeled out of his hymn fragment *As on a Day of Festivity*, or in this case, taken out of the now familiar context, through the phrase "But oh, where from", which returns in *Half of Life* as a contrasting "But oh, where do I take […]". Schmidt stressed that the celebratory anthem breaks off "in the middle of the attempt to shape the existential problem of poetic *mediation*. The poet's difficulty is to convey the vastness, fullness and intensity of the context of life experienced in nature and history to the narrow and meagre existence of man […]".

Does the large number of versions and drafts that are known to accumulate in Hölderlin's late period speak for the poet's growing insecurity and doubts about his own approach or, more precisely, for his attempts to find solutions to this acute problem of mediation? Is Schmidt right when he says: "Even the latest hymns reveal how much Hölderlin struggled to counter the idealistic danger of setting or suggesting meanings that rush, or even miss the objective course of history"?

For Hölderlin, "sense" meant revelation through the "heavenly". "As if on a day of festivity" breaks off at the point where this revelation threatens to topple:

I approached to behold the heavenly ones,
They themselves, they cast me deep down among the living
The fake priest, in the dark, that I
Sing the warning song to those who want to learn.
There ...

(Ich sei genaht, die Himmlischen zu schauen,
Sie selbst, sie werfen mich tief unter die Lebenden
Den falschen Priester, ins Dunkel, daß ich
Das warnende Lied den Gelehrigen singe.
Dort ...)

Here, the following questions arise: Does the poet see himself as a "false priest"? Is the "darkness"—as is well known one of the common characteristics when dealing with Hölderlin's late poems—a necessary condition for singing the "warning song" from "there"? Who are "those who want to learn"? Are they considered the intelligent ones and thus the select few among the "living"? And why do the "celestial ones" "throw" the poet down at all? Do they sense his competition?

No, a "mad project" could by no means be deduced from this, as tempting as Lange's assumption was at first glance. Later, in his study of *Hölderlin's Historical-Philosophical Hymns* (1990), Schmidt showed how the triadic form was able to stabilize the precarious interrelationship between (failed) self-empowerment on the one hand and self-confidence ("Woe is me") on the other, at least in the valid versions of the poems *Celebration of Peace, The Only One*, and *Patmos*. But then, had Hölderlin tried to develop a philosophically and poetically proven view of historical developments after all?

Once again, further research on Hölderlin focused on the poem *Half of Life*. Winfried Menninghaus took it as the occasion for a concise and circumspect *Essay on Hölderlin's Poetics* (2005), whereby he was able to offer fundamentally new insights into what must probably be the most intensively interpreted fourteen lines of German-language poetry. Based on a subtle metrical analysis, he also took Hölderlin's use of the Sapphic Adoneus as the "metrical signature of the poem" seriously, in terms of content, and felt that Sappho and the Sapphic were a core inspiration for Hölderlin. He was able to emphasize "Sappho" and "Diotima" as the "position of a female authority in the symbolic". Hölderlin's ideal of beauty, the motif of sexual transgression presumably based on life experience, but above all the erotic moment in his poetry thus gained a new dimension with a considerable poetic consequence: Hölderlin's interest in Sappho, his Sapphism, if you will, relativized the supposed pre-eminent Pindaric which, with its "hard", that is "masculine", metric constructions, was long understood as *the* defining characteristic of his late poetry. Menninghaus's findings are compelling: "Hölderlin could only become a master of hard structures because he knew all the secrets of the sweet and soft constructions and never completely "denied" them in his late language, but even intensified them in contrast". Moreover, Menninghaus refers to a central connection in the aftermath of Hölderlin and his interpreters that deserves to be quoted in full:

Nietzsche, a clairvoyant admirer of Hölderlin long before the great editorial and scientific efforts of the twentieth century began, still noticed as a matter of course, in addition to the "joint waving in the most sublime swing of the odes " a "losing oneself in the most delicate sounds of melancholy" and ultimately saw both poles as "welling with the purest, softest mind". [...] Hellingrath, too, did not fail to recognize the "swelling sweet sobbing or melting of the odes" in addition to the "hard verse construction". However, by declaring the great pindarizing poems to be Hölderlin's "real legacy" and interpreting them as the "Word of God" in "hard verses", he broke the path of a comprehensive recoding of Hölderlin, at the end of which the Sapphic "female" part has largely disappeared behind the forced role of the male herald. In Hölderlin's previously extremely 'soft' image, the cult of masculinity of the George circle has thus left a strikingly strong and lasting mark. Without this symbolic gender reassignment, Hölderlin would probably not have become a paperback companion of German soldiers so easily.

At times, one should remember the long and sometimes rocky road Hölderlin research has taken until it was able to find such sophisticated controversies and insights, let us say since the *Musenalmanach for the Year 1807*, in which Leo von Seckendorf published the first verse of *Bread and Wine* under the title "The Night" with the best of intentions and with a sharp eye for "beautiful passages", but the following year, he provided a platform for the hymns *The Rhine*, *Patmos* and *Remembrance*. Hölderlin probably no longer took notice of these. For by this time, he had already become the main victim of his inner polarities. His sensitivity and ability had come up against the "hard constructions" of fate.

The merit of Menninghaus' reflections on *Half of Life* also lies in the fact that they include questions related to artistic productivity. As in the case of Jochen Schmidt, they are as much about the *how* as they are about the *why* of this type of poetry. Hölderlin *wanted to* distance himself from the contemporary way of writing poetry and to elevate poetry to the "*mechane of* the ancients". For "the modern poetry is particularly lacking in the schooling and craftsmanship, namely that its mode of procedure is calculated and taught, and when it is learned, can be reliably repeated again and again in practice". And it was precisely with, and through, this approach that Hölderlin wanted to protect himself from the threat of "madness".

In spite of all the controversies, however, there are now generally accepted positions of research and interpretation that affect Hölderlin's sources as much as his poetological stance. "Aesthetics of expression" was not his thing. "With his poetics and its implementation, he questions the conception of poetry that is oriented towards self-expression and, what is even more radical, opposes any aesthetics that are oriented towards expression with a poetics of representation" (Rainer Nägele). Hölderlin was unquestionably on the way to a "philosophy of composition" in the literal sense of Edgar A. Poe.

Hölderlin research has long since become an international phenomenon, and while these remarks on its "status" can only be partial, we would like to refer to outstanding examples of translational and philological achievements, especially in the Anglophone world: From Michael Hamburger, David Gascoyne, John Riley, Cyrus Hamlin to David Constantine and Christopher Middleton, as far as the translation and interpretation of the poems is concerned; Jeremy Adler and Charlie Louth, who have succeeded in effectively translating Hölderlin's central letter-work and poetic essays into English; Howard Gaskill's investigations into *Hyperion* and the *Celebration of Peace*; Mark Ogden's study *The Problem of Christ in the Work of Friedrich Hölderlin* (1991) and Ian Cooper's comparative work *The Near and Distant God. Poetry, Idealism and Religious Thought from Hölderlin to Eliot* (2008). The most important study on *The Poet as Thinker: Hölderlin in France* (1994), however, is owed to a Belgian scholar, Geert Lernout. Of particular note, however, is a pioneering study that Marshall Montgomery presented in two volumes under the title *Friedrich Hölderlin and the German Neo-Hellenic*

Movement in 1923. The foreword, in which the author refers to Karl Breul as Hölderlin's first mediator in England, and to the fact that Montgomery was able to obtain books from the Giessen University Library in Oxford in the years 1914–19 (!!), is significant in the History of Science.

Occasionally it can happen that the new edition of translations contributes to a media-oriented, almost global reevaluation of Hölderlin, as happened when Michael Hamburger's collected Hölderlin translations into English were published, and the South African-Australian Nobel Prize winner for literature, John Maxwell Coetzee, contributed a six-page biographical essay on "The Poet in the Tower" in *The New York Review of Books* (2006). He began his attempt with a poem written in London by the young exile Michael Hamburger in the middle of World War II, a lament in an English language that was as close to Hölderlin's tonalities as Hölderlin's poems were to Greek: "Diotima is dead, and silent/The island's singing bird/The temple I raised from ruin/Fallen again./Where is the flame I stoked from ashes/Of the mind? Where are the heroes/And my pulsing song?/Nothing stirs on the lakes of time". With this poem and others in this tonality, so to speak, Hamburger had prepared himself for one of his great tasks in life, to present Hölderlin in English as a poetic event.

If taken together, these creative engagements with Hölderlin amount to nothing less than a celebration of this poet in the English language, a language that has become poetically richer for it as did the original German through the uniqueness of Hölderlin's poetic register.

"Remembering Floating Hölderlin Towers" or: Writing Hölderlin

With the expression *le pauvre Holterling*, Countess Caroline von Hessen-Homburg introduced a letter, probably written to her daughter on 13 September 1806, in which she told her how the sometimes raving, sometimes frightened poet had to be taken away from Homburg in the direction of Tübingen. With this, however, the poet became the subject of rumors and, later, of poetry itself. The English surrealist David Gascoyne was supposed to overcome his writing crisis in France in 1937/38 with a short cycle, which he gave the title *Hölderlin's Madness*, in which a figure appears in a landscape with limbs. This figure describes her nakedness as the only possible armour against the attacks of the time. And Jean Tardieu, in a poem from 1954, *Le Tombeau de Hölderlin* (*Hölderlin's Tomb*), hopes that "the times will mix" and that "out of the tumult/a single voice will emerge, quietly/dominating the thunder, and that smile/stronger than the elements earthly struggle". Even more strongly than

Gascoyne, Samuel Beckett reveals the phenomenon of a hidden engagement with Hölderlin, whose philosophical scope, problems of connection, and rich contradictions, between the ontologically conditioned poetry (Hölderlin) and expressions of radical negation (Beckett), Dieter Henrich has examined. Beckett's Hölderlin edition, richly annotated, is kept in the Reading University Library. When the young Beckett read *Hyperion* in 1938, he noted in the margin: "fit for *Das I.R.* [Innere Reich]", thus establishing a connection between the central journalistic organ of the so-called Inner Emigration, from and within Hitlerism, and Hölderlin's world of thought and style. In addition, he recognized, as can be seen from a letter written in April 1951, that in the thinking of Heidegger and Maurice Blanchot, whose essay "La parole "sacrée" de Hölderlin" (1946) Beckett had read at the time, everything imprecise had to be "paid for by poor Hölderlin". Anne Atik reported that Beckett and her later husband, the Romanian-Israeli artist Avigdor Arikha, recited whilst standing Hölderlin verses such as: "Many have died/Commanders in olden days/And beautiful women and poets/And in newer/Of men many,/But I am alone". Moreover, both friends would have been "ecstatic about the ungrammatical miracle" of the Hölderlin verse "But not it is/The time". In his miniature poems *Trötentönen (Mirlitonnades)*, written around 1977, Beckett recorded a poem that could even be read as a parody of Hölderlin's Elegy *Stuttgart*: "In Stuttgart, do not miss/looking at the long Neckarstrasse./The attraction of nothingness there is no longer what it once was,/because one just/has the very strong suspicion/of having been in the middle of it for a long time."

Le pauvre Holterling—above every poem dedicated to the memory of Hölderlin this phrase seems to be written with invisible ink. "Come upwards,/Pitied saint!/Look up/With your errant eye,/With the beauty of your youth,/From the open misty grave/Of your childlike heart." Thus Wilhelm Waiblinger's hymn *An Hölderlin* from 1823, begins. A decade earlier, in mid-April 1812, Ernst Zimmer, the Tübingen carpenter, landlord and innkeeper of the tower room with the bay window, writes to Hölderlin's mother:

His poetic spirit is still active, so he saw a drawing of a temple with me. He told me I should make one of wood like this, I replied to him that I would have to work for my bread, as I was not as happy to live in philosophical peace as he is, to which he immediately said, Oh, I am a wretched man, and in the very same minute he wrote the following verse with pencil on a board

> The lines of life are different
> As paths are and the edges of mountains.
> What Here we are, a God can match over there
> With harmonies and eternal reward and peace.

(Die Linien des Lebens sind Verschieden
Wie Wege sind, und wie der Berge Gränzen.
Was Hir wir sind, kan dort ein Gott ergänzen
Mit Harmonien und ewigem Lohn und Frieden.)

When and under what circumstances does a real situation become literary? Four years earlier, the poet and medic, Justinus Kerner, had led his Berlin visitor, *homme de lettres* Karl August Varnhagen von Ense, to this "wretched man". Varnhagen noted down after reading Hölderlin's translations of Sophocles that he thought they were "pretty amazing, but only so in literary terms, something which one takes very far in our country without being insane or being taken for such". Moreover, he had a "double novel" in mind, in which a translator named Wacholder would have featured, "who was to become like Hölderlin's Sophocles "—in other words, a translator who would become his own model. "It was only by chance that it didn't happen, and only the better for my sake... For it would be a terrible thought to have mocked a lunatic, as ghastly as wanting to beat a corpse." And again the cry: "Poor Hölderlin!"—in the face of his "crazy talking," a "stream of words," though without "peculiar thoughts" or "witty deduction." He was still regarded as strikingly "beautiful"; the mind, not the body, seemed worn. It appeared that he did not like to tolerate silence; he needed language. As it was said in the *Wanderer-Elegy* (1800/01): "And the speech drove me to search for something else./Far to the north pole I came up in ships./…where the bound life quietly slept in a shell of snow… and the iron sleep awaited for years the day" ("Und es trieb die Rede mich an, noch andres zu suchen./Fern zum nördlichen Pol kam ich in Schiffen herauf./Still in der Hülse von Schnee schlief da das gefesselte Leben,/Und der eiserne Schlaf harrte seit Jahren des Tags."). To awaken and unleash the sleeping nature, that is what looked like an ideal to him.

What happened to this way of "talking"? The poem *Tübingen, Jänner (Tübingen, January)* (1963) by Paul Celan can be read as a response. Even if no modern poem on Hölderlin is better known than this one, it should be quoted in full:

Tübingen, Jänner (Tübingen, January)

Eyes talked into
Blindness.
Their – "an enigma is
that of the pure
origin"—, their
memory of
Hölderlin's towers afloat, circled
by whirring gulls.

Visits of drowned joiners to
These
submerging words:

Should,
should a man,
should a man come into the world, today, with
the shining beard of the
patriarchs: he could
if he spoke of this
time, he
could
only babble and babble
over, over
again again.

("Pallaksch. Pallaksch.")

What is this? A double parody of the poem *Half of Life* and the *Rhine* hymn, in which the phrase "drunk with kisses" strangely enough turns into "drowned joiners", and instead of the swans dipping their heads into "holy sober water" becomes "submerging" or diving words? And in double refraction the enigmatic sentence from Hölderlin's hymn returns: "An enigma is that of pure origin."

A prerequisite of Celan's poem is that it is the inner eye, which sees all this. Because before the poem begins, (many?) words had to be used to "persuade" the eyes to let their light go out. What follows are repeated attempts to be able to say what remains to be said, *slurred* by the state of the times, to say in Hölderlin's word of self-renunciation or self-denial: *Pallaksch*, a magic word that suspends meaning and significance. This would be the case even if a person appeared with all the signs of a wise man, engaged in enlightening people, with their emblematically "shining beard of the patriarchs".

Johannes Bobrowski, the poet who is particularly associated with Klopstock and Hölderlin, reminds us of the existential weight of this poetry with an alienating allusion to—once again—the poem *Half of Life* (in *Hölderlin in Tübingen*): "It is difficult to weigh the heaviness/against the greenery,/trees and water,/both in one hand:/the bell rings down/over the roofs, the clock/stirs with the turning/of iron flags."

The poems from the anthology *An Hölderlin* (1993) often consist of set pieces from his work, but some of them want to demonstrate just how much lyricists "need" him again in our "meagre times". "May you be, singing, my friendly asylum". "From where do I take…". Longing for the Garonne. Or in Erich Fried's reversal that celebrates the becoming of ambiguity and demands: "Never again/Only signs, without meaning." Or like Arnfried Astel: "I have heard people talk about/Hölderlin who/would not have talked to him/. I do not/want to talk to them." In "Madness/of the Neckar/baptized", this is how Rose Ausländer sees her Hölderlin. By contrast, Erich Fried displays a rare intensity in his poetic and political engagement with

Hölderlin, (How very differently did his fellow exile, Michael Hamburger, react to Hölderlin, namely almost emphatically in a non-political way.) Peter Rühmkorf and Hans Magnus Enzensberger, on the other hand, followed Fried's example and varied the *Song of the German*, quite literally as Wolf Biermann did in his "Hölderlin song" with the line that became famous: "In this country we live/like strangers in our own house/We do not understand our own language, how it strikes us/nor do we understand what we say/who speaks our language/In this country we live like strangers", thought as a variation on the *Hyperion* line: "That's how I came among the Germans".

Time and again poetic minds, as well as literary critics like Marcel Reich-Ranicki, rub against one of Hölderlin's comparatively weak but undoubtedly effective poems, *Death for the Fatherland* (*Der Tod fürs Vaterland*, 1797/99). They find it difficult not to reconcile with the poet's later *Celebration of Peace*, but rather with his fundamental examination of the German character and the "Homeland" in numerous works from this very period, most notably in Hyperion's vitriolic criticism of "the Germans". Wolf Biermann had titled his interpretation of the ode, which was based on Horace and Klopstock, with the question "Fatherland phrases or a Swabian Marseillaise?" and began as follows "Hardly surprising that the Nazis were delighted. Chauvinist high school teachers celebrated these words to the children they sent to Hitler's lost war." He read the text "in an anthology for soldiers of Hölderlin's works, procured by Friedrich Beißner, a lyrical front parcel, an iron ration for the soldiers of the Wehrmacht, so that death for the fatherland would be easier for them." In the end, Biermann concedes that this ode was meant "as a German, a Württemberg Marseillaise". He realizes that it was about the struggle for freedom. But what really bothered him about this poem was its "stench of excitement." This was written in early autumn 1991. A few months earlier, at an event organized by the Hölderlin Society to mark the 148th anniversary of the poet's death, he had described the ode as a "drunken celebration of the victim's death" and as "warmongering trash". In tone, this sounded even more garish than that which the then star of German literary reviewers, Reich-Ranicki, had printed on 27 June 1987, as a laudatory speech for Peter Härtling on the occasion of the presentation of the Hölderlin Prize ("No, I do not love him, this Friedrich Hölderlin."). *Death for the Fatherland*, Reich-Ranicki said on this occasion, was the work of a "desk offender". Once again, Jochen Schmidt must be agreed with when he described this ode as what it wanted to be: A "revolutionary appeal calling for a fight against the oppressors at home", i.e. the autocratic sovereigns who trampled on civil rights and sold their "children of the state" as mercenaries. In a draft of this ode, Hölderlin wrote "For those who called themselves fathers to him [the child of the country],/They are thieves,/Who stole the child/From the cradle/And deceived the pious heart of the child,/Like a tame animal, used for service." ("Denn die sich Väter ihm [dem Landeskind, R.G.] nannten,/Diebe sind sie,/Die den Deutschen das Kind/Aus der Wiege gestohlen/Und das fromme Herz des Kindes betrogen,/ /Wie ein zahmes Thier, zum Dienste gebraucht.")

There is one thing, however, that the enraged readers of this poem seem to persistently overlook: The persona of this ode is a spectator, or onlooker, reporting on what is happening before his eyes in the manner of a classical teichoscopy. He wants to belong, but sees himself as a "minor/stranger". Explaining the background to this seemingly notorious poem, Günter Mieth refers to a biographical fact. "Fleeing from the advancing Sambre-Meuse army, Hölderlin comes to Bad Driburg as an escort to the Gontard family and lives probably only half an hour away from the valley "where Hermann defeated the legions of Varus", as he writes to his brother on 3 October 1796." It is conceivable that this experience was especially marked by the presence of Susette Gontard, who is said to have known, from her Hamburg days, "the poet Klopstock personally." In conversation with her lover, given the precariousness of their situation, she may have reminded Hölderlin of Klopstock's "Song of the Fatherland" of 1749, in which he glorified the Prussian King Frederick the Great. Thus, this ode may also have been the result of (contemporary) historical transitions. Hölderlin's work is not easy to come by with coarsening theses, whether they are journalistically or poetically motivated.

Incidentally, Reich-Ranicki's controversial intervention in Hölderlin's case had a curious and conciliatory aftermath: He was awarded the Hölderlin Prize in 2000 and the then Federal Minister of State for Culture Michael Naumann was called upon to remind people that the critic's love of poetry and his suffering for Germany were closely related. After all, the prizewinner had put on record that Hölderlin's *Half of Life* was "unsurpassed" and his ode *To the Fates* (*An die Parzen*) was among the "wonders of the German language". It was impossible "not to admire Friedrich Hölderlin", and difficult, Ranicki conceded, "not to venerate him". After all, Reich-Ranicki had Hölderlin's poems discussed thirty-three times for his legendary *Frankfurt Anthology*, which he later published as a separate anthology of Hölderlin's poems with interpretations under the title *And Full of Wild Roses.*

The speeches given at Hölderlin Award ceremonies have become a barometer for the poetic-intellectual climate, which of course also applies to those delivered in the name of other classics. "And the wise/Often, in the end, lean towards the beautiful" ("Und es neigen die Weisen/Oft am Ende zu Schönem sich"), one might say with the final verses of Hölderlin's poem *Socrates and Alcibiades*. On one such occasion, in 2006, Rüdiger Safranski described Hölderlin as a "meteor of the night of the gods, which no one felt more deeply". The prelude to his speech addressed the problem of understanding, which he also shared with Martin Walser, but first Safranski's—furious and prudent—prelude, if there is such a thing:

Just as we hold our heads or hearts with every attempt to understand Hölderlin in panic and amazement in the face of such great and beautiful strangeness, so Hölderlin himself was frightened by himself or marvelled at himself, or more precisely: at what he wrote about. He was not only frightened and astonished, he was also full of melancholy and despair at the fact that the very moment of writing poetry, and the world that opened up to him as a result, passed away again.

What is poetry, what is reflected *in* us? What is it that poetry allows to express? Ten years earlier, Martin Walser had emphasized the "use" of Hölderlin's poetry and thus directly responded to the poet's despair that no one had any use for him in his time. But he also referred to the fact that Hölderlin condemned as "hypocritical" those poets who had the word "gods" in their mouths without believing in them. Walser asked: "What, then, does it mean to have the most sacred lines in one's mouth all through life?" That they are sacred lines, one should never doubt. Safranski, by and large, shared this view. But Reich-Ranicki argued: "A poetry with such inflationary use of the word "sacred" should not be accepted without contradiction."

It is, then, quite fitting to find that one of Walser's sons-in-law, the writer Karl-Heinz Ott, offered a partisan reading of Hölderlin and the "ghosts" (2019) he unleashed in the 20th century. But with this attempt to deconstruct Hölderlin and his legacy Ott seems to be oblivious to the fact that, in so doing, he turns into one of the Hölderlinian "ghosts" himself.

In his "theological aesthetics" (*Gloriousness*, 1962) Hans Urs von Balthasar gave Hölderlin's poetry a central role and claimed that "holy" in Hölderlin's work referred to the presence of the "eternal spirit". But the Hölderlin Award speeches also allow for this, especially given the lauditory nature of the responses. They mainly offer attributions, the pointing out of rather subliminal connections between the award-winner and the eponym. This happened, for example, in Jochen Hieber's speech on the poet Doris Runge, about whose poems he wrote that although they "avoid the high tone of Hölderlin's great hymns and elegies" as well as the "far-reaching tails of images and arcs of thought", and thus do not have the same effect, some things in her work are reminiscent of Hölderlin's fragments, or more precisely, of those germ words and fragments that he wrote down in order to expand them later, which then remained separate and often form a coherent, sometimes highly modern and open-ended, whole within themselves. Hieber, who had clearly raised the level of journalistic responses to Hölderlin with his important article on the one hundred and fiftieth anniversary of the poet's death, juxtaposes the fragment "To my sister" with Runge's poem "ländlich" ("rural") from the volume *kommt zeit* (*time will tell*, 1988). First, Hölderlin's fragment:

When I stay overnight in the village

air from the Swabian mountains

down the road

House Seeing again. Sun of the
    Homeland

Boat ride,
...friends, men and mother.
Slumber

(Übernacht ich im Dorf

Albluft
 Straße hinunter

Haus Wiedersehn. Sonne der
    Heimath

Kahnfahrt,
freunde Männer und Mutter.
Schlummer)

Runge's poetic response

a window seat
with a view to the future
cleaned and raked
the track
of the boxwood
soft hills
flowers
in beautiful succession
it's getting dark earlier and earlier

A correspondence to Hölderlin's musicality and the floating (Walser had referred to the "floating emphasis" in Hölderlin's Alcaic verse) with "all failure and disappearance" is discovered by the critic and laudator in Runge's poem "pas de deux" ("step of two"):

> change
> step and
> forth and
> back and forth
> and turn
> pair disappears
> image remains still

It was no coincidence that Safranski ended his speech by referring to Hölderlin's disappearance in a "picture" (meaning our "image" of him). It was known that a copy of *Hyperion* lay open on his table almost all these years [during Hölderlin's benighted life "in the tower"] and he dived into it as if he wanted to disappear in it.

But let us pause once again and reflect the sheer intensity that could result from the poetic confrontation with Hölderlin at the very beginning of the First World War, but this time without any chauvinistic derailments. Yet, the author of this hymnic-elegiac poem, Rainer Maria Rilke, was himself in danger of such "derailing" only a month earlier (in August 1914), with his martial *Five Songs*; for they owed their existence partly to Rilke's reading of Hölderlin's hymns. But this homage to Hölderlin was of a different, suitably sublime kind:

To Hölderlin

We are not permitted to linger, even with what is most
familiar. From images that are full, the spirit's
stream plunges down to others that suddenly must be filled;
there are no lakes till eternity. Here, falling
is ablest. To fall from the mastered emotion
into the guessed-at, and onwards.

To you, O majestic poet, to you the compelling image,
O caster of spells, was a life, entire; when you uttered it
a line snapped shut like fate; there was a death
even in the mildest, and you entered it; but
the god who preceded you led you out and beyond it,
O wandering spirit, most wandering of all! How snugly
the others live in their warming poems, homely, and stay
content, in their narrow similes. Taking part. Only you
move like the moon. And beneath, the nocturnal landscape
brightens and darkens—your sacred, your terrified landscape,
which you feel in departures. No one
gave it away more sublimely, gave it back to the universe
more fully, without any need to hold on. So also,
for years that you no longer counted, holy, you played
with infinite joy, as though it were not inside you, but lay
belonging to no one, all around
on the gentle lawns of the earth, where the godlike children had left it.

Ah, you built what the loftiest spirits have longed for:
free of desire, you laid it, stone upon stone,
till it stood. And when it collapsed, even then
you weren't bewildered.

Why, after such an eternal man lived, do we still
lack faith in the earthly? and not reverently learn from transience
the emotions for what future
slopes of the heart, in pure space?

Rilke's answer to Hölderlin was, as mentioned, made possible by the publication of the late hymns in volume four of Hellingrath's edition of his works. In a letter from that time, Rilke speaks of fragments of Hölderlin whose beauty "makes one think of the poems of Sappho" (!). This hymn by Rilke ascribes a prophetic significance to the great ancestor of lyrical modernism, which incidentally Gustav Landauer was to connect with the Jewish tradition of prophesizing in a lecture in 1916. But this prophecy leads us to observe two features of this poem: Firstly, Rilke's hymn alludes to the constant movement in Hölderlin, who set his course because it was that of his heart, as Rilke emphasized himself in the letter in question. But, secondly, this poetic "star" does not shine from within itself, but is a "moon" illuminated by important traditions, a "moon" which, of course, also knows how to illuminate and darken. Tumbling, falling, even "overthrow", are contrasting with this poet who unswervingly follows his path. In contrast to the previous examples, these moments of movement determine the image of Hölderlin that Rilke creates for, and through, this hymn. This poetry does not allow the reader to "linger"; and indeed, it is primarily rhythmic, through the walking and naming of transitional stages in culture and history and through those often contradictory emotional movements that characterize Hölderlin's poetry.

Even though Rilke's poem is a more well-known "consequence" of the rediscovery of Hölderlin after 1900 it is by no means the only one. Another comes in the form of a lyric response by a poet of the time, Georg Trakl. As mentioned in the introduction, the poem, written in 1910, was only discovered quite recently (2016). Trakl had entered it into his copy of Wilhelm Böhm's edition of Hölderlins works (1905), which included his drama *Empedocles* as well as his Sophocles translations (*Antigone* and *Oedipus*).

> Hölderlin
>
> The forest is spreading out autumnally,
> The winds are resting not to wake him.
> The game sleeps peacefully in hideaways,
> whilst the brook is gliding very quietly.
>
> A noble mind was darkened thus
> In all lustre and mourn of its beauty
> By mania as whispered by a pious shiver
> through the herbs on some eve.

After the initial pastoral, the second stanza refers to "mania", or madness, that seems entirely in tune with nature. The allusion to Ophelia's words about Hamlet ("O, what a noble mind is here o'erthrown") is obvious, but rendered in a somewhat mellowed fashion. In the original, the rhyme structure (abba) suggests a self-contained poetic essence. In it, "mourning" and "shiver" ("Trauer" and "Schauer") belong as much together as "to wake" and "hideaways" ("wecken" and "Verstecken"). The state of madness is seen as the poet's second nature, as it were. There is nothing disturbing about it; rather, it is consequential given the intimacy between the poet and nature. The absence of any other person in this poem suggests that the only genuine communication occurs between the pastoral and the one possessed by mania, for whom "Hölderlin" is but a name, interchangeable with any other, including "Scardanelli".

"I would like to/live hand in hand with Scardanelli", we read in Friederike Mayröcker's work, and thus in the work of an Austrian poetess of our time, which seems to be heading straight for this dual identity called Hölderlin/Scardanelli. "Be thou with me in my language madness", she asks or demands, invoking the presence of her life-death companion. "Hölderlin Tower, on the Neckar, in May" is the title of the opening poem of her volume *Scardanelli* (2009), which dates from 1989: "I open a window/in the garden you say the trees/are still the same as they were then". At that time Hölderlin was merely an occasional companion. After the death of Ernst Jandl (2000), on 9 June, incidentally, two days after the day Hölderlin died, the two poets seemed to have joined forces in the perception of her memory. But when she went "hand in hand" with Scardanelli in 2009, a critic even spoke of Mayröcker's "downright tender infidelity" towards her "heart's companion"

Ernst Jandl. Traces of Hölderlin can also be found, for example, in her volume *My Worktyrol (Mein Arbeitstirol*, 2003), where she makes a verse line of a fragment her own: *"'You safely constructed Alps', Hölderlin"*. The poem seems to have nothing in common with the original, except for the use of the word "Namely", subordinated in Hölderlin's manner. At any rate, the following verse sequence reveals a deeper relationship dimension:

> [...] In dreams today your waving from afar, slightly
> covered by strange shapes I don't know, entered
> into another world or sank into the abyss
> of nothingness? No longer knowing of you of me of
> the milky earth with stigmata and
> larch woods blessed us, back then ... you will
> wake up, you say, in tears, and one poem
> that has written itself will lie next to you
> on the pillow – will ever rise you again? Will
> we see each other again?

What is meant are "notches of love" of a surviving Diotima, whereby the poem, which writes itself, refers to an autopoetic constellation: The dream triggers a sensory fantasy that verbally refers to the unknown, but with both questions touching on something very personal. Mayröcker's recurring image of the poet standing at the window seems related to Scardanelli's view of the river landscape from his tower room window, even if Mayröcker's perspective is not explicitly related to Tübingen: "Musical thunderstorm in front of my windows, Vienna", Mayröcker noted in her prose *The Heart-Rending of Things* (*Das Herzzerreißende der Dinge*, 1985). This thunderstorm proves not to be divinely wrathful, but rather brings the yearning desire of this persona to visit the house of the beloved in his absence, whereby this emotional impulse leads to a decidedly abstract question, which can also concern her way of engaging with

Hölderlin: "I ask myself, is the striving for the realization of a modernity accessible to all something utopian?"

Since then we have entered the era of travel restrictions, social distancing, self-isolation, suspicion, anxieties, collective (media) hysteria, amounting to unprecedented curtailing of civil liberties in the name of public health in a world dominated by Covid-19. Small wonder that one of the foremost contemporary German-language poets, Ilma Rakusa, would offer a large-scale elegiac poem with the title "Corona with Hölderlin" (2020). Intercepted by quotations from Hölderlin, Rakusa's poem works with "breath", or "pneumà" as one of his and her key-motifs: "We need breath protection/In order to survive". To a certain extent, Rakusa's poem is an extended set of variations on Hölderlin's theme "But where danger looms,/What can save us will grow, too", from his hymn *Patmos*, which in itself testified to the life-giving power of breath. But Rakusa's "Corona with Hölderlin" also asks the question whether the "saving grace" might contain "danger", too, surely a concern that will continue to bedevil us for an unspecifiable time to come.

"[…] but soon we will be but a song": Musical Reflections of Hölderlin

With Johannes Brahms, the serious compositional engagement with Hölderlin's work began. His setting of Hyperion's *Schicksalslied* (op. 54) for choir and orchestra (1871) was the important prelude to a development which, with long interruptions, extends into the post-atonal present. But to begin with, one should pay attention to the musical foundation of Hölderlin's poems itself, which is evident above all in their rhythmic structures, but also in the way they thematize the subject of "singing" and "song".

Silence and singing—can an "alliance" between the two succeed? Hölderlin's *Celebration of Peace* hints in the preface that its language conjures up a certain "Sangart" or mode of "singing". And later, it expresses the conviction that people will develop from "conversation" to "singing".

Singing is a fundamental word in the work of this music-loving poet. There is hardly one of his poems that could not be described as singing or displaying an affinity to music.

And yet it is striking that only one of his poem titles uses the actual word "Gesang", the German word for "song". At the end of the *Patmos* hymn it is again "German song" that will, or should, follow the "good interpretation" of existing by means of "fixed letter(s)".

Hölderlin's birthday ode (1799) for his patroness, Princess Auguste of Homburg, concludes with the hope: "O that from this joyous day my time/may begin, that at last a song may also/thrive for me in your groves,/Noble One! worthy of you." ("O daß von diesem freudigen Tage mir/Auch meine Zeit beginne, daß endlich auch/Mir ein Gesang in deinen Hainen,/Edle! Gedeihe, der deiner wert sei.") The democratic aspect of poems is that in it, even royalty can be addressed as "you".

In the *Song of the Germans*, which uses an Alkaic metre, Hölderlin sought after the Greek element in German culture ("Do you know Minerva's children? [...] Where is your Delos, where is your Olympia?"), ("Kennst du Minervas Kinder? [...] Wo ist dein Delos, wo dein Olympia?"), a verse (the fifth), illustrates what the "beautiful" is all about, which could be withheld from the poetic persona, which is, as always, on the margins, had it not been involved in this "Fatherland":

> By your streams I walked and conceiving you,
> Meanwhile the notes shy the nightingale
> In the rough pasture sang, and in silence
> On dawning ground the wave dwelt.

(An deinen Strömen ging ich und dachte dich,
Indes die Töne schüchtern die Nachtigall
Auf schwanker Weide sang, und still auf
Dämmerndem Grunde die Welle weilte.)

What sounds restrained here is also meant to be reflexive. The verse is far from that "rejoicing madness" that "seizes the singers on holy night" and makes the lyrical "I" demand to reach the "Isthmos" "where the open sea roars". But both noises refer to the foundation of Hölderlin's "singing", the sounds of nature, which are, however, poetically brought into form. Hölderlin rarely uses alliteration. Here, the dwelling of the wave signals a thoughtful flowing of his native rivers. It does not rush and thus not disturb the hesitant song of the nightingale. It remains audible despite the bird's untypical "shyness". What prevails is the song, even if it does not seem powerful.

But matters can also be different: "I want to sing lightly, but I never succeed, because my happiness never makes speech [light] for me." ("Singen wollt ich leichten Gesang, doch nimmer gelingt mirs,/Denn [es] machet mein Glück nimmer die Rede mir [leicht].") One has suspected that Hölderlin's self-critical insight prevented the completion of the elegy *Walk to the Country* (Sattler/Schmitz). The emphasis here, of course, is on the *light* singing, which is contrasted by the heaviness of "happiness"–in the sense of the *Germania* hymn.

Through the way in which "Gesang" ("song") is used in Hölderlin's poems, this very concept comes across as multi-layered, *polysonar*, i.e. multi-resonant. It can be "flotsam" as in the fragment "Like sea coasts" or "unholy" with every sound, depending on how Hölderlin relates the disposition of the "singer". After all, it is the latter on whom the reconciliation between natural sounds and artistic singing depends. The singing can be a "bridal song of heaven" (in the fragment "The Vatican") or it can be composed of the voices of "the people" or "fate", possibly interspersed with "gentle swallow cries" or "the song of the blackbird". Even "clouds of song" can imagine these poems ("Greece—Second Approach"). But there is one attribute that Hölderlin ascribed to song, and in the ongoing debate about his late work, much points in this direction: the "fortified" nature of song. It can be found in the hymn fragment "From the Abyss Namely", in the approach to a poetry that—according to everything that has been said—would have celebrated the sensual experience, had it been completed. One sensual metaphor follows the other. In it, there is talk of being drunk with light, of the "sharp odour" that "blows around the holes in the rock", of the "scent of lemon" and a berry that hangs "like coral" from the bush. And in the midst of this celebration of the senses and their perception up to the pain threshold, is found the half verse: "[…] fortified song of flowers as/New formation from the city where […]" ("[…] befestigter Gesang von Blumen als/Neue Bildung aus der Stadt, wo […]".). It is this "settled song" that once again divides the editorial minds. Dieter Uffhausen has isolated the expression and in his edition of "hymnic late poetry until 1806" (1989/90) has elevated it to its main title. On the part of established Hölderlin philology, this treatment of the "consolidated song" was answered with out-of-tune, if not shrill dissonant criticism, namely by Dieter Burdorf. The case is once again of a principled nature and ties in with the editorial controversies discussed earlier. The prepositional structure "von Blumen" is indeed written in Hölderlin's Homburg folio booklet as an addition on the right margin; Uffhausen does not consider its generally accepted assignment to "fortified song" to be compelling. Gerhard Kurz, however, argued that at this point the "song of the poet takes up the song that nature already sings and connects it with an "education" that he owes to the "city" […] From the city the new song goes out as a 'fortified song of flowers'". Burdorf, who takes Uffhausen's way of representation to task, offers a conciliatory thesis by asserting that Hölderlin's late poetic fragments contain "a communicative impulse before which any monological editorial or interpretive procedure that levels the multi-dimensionality of the text and excludes the variety of competing readings proves to be false".

Beyond these philological problems, Hölderlin's "singing" realizes "musical relations" that convey nature and culture, and this in the form of poetic "acoustic figures" (Novalis). Their characteristic feature is a poetics of alternating tones and rhythms, which Hölderlin himself gave its most concise designation with the term "harmonic opposite". To see in this, with Rainer Nägele, an anticipation of the thesis of the musical foundation of being by the early Friedrich Nietzsche, seems more than admissible.

Attention was given to the question of what Hölderlin's concrete musical experience had actually consisted of. The instrument important to him was the flute. An encounter with the blind flute virtuoso Friedrich Ludwig Dülon (of similar age), is credibly recorded in the summer of 1788.

But we also know that the sixteen-year-old student wanted to master the "Clavier" in Maulbronn in order to be able to play the songs from Schiller's drama *Die Räuber* set to music by Johann Rudolf Zumsteeg. Schiller's thesis that a musical mood precedes the poetic production could have been counter-signed by Hölderlin, too, and not only in this early phase. But nothing else is known about Hölderlin's musical repertoire. The art of improvisation seems to have suited him, also, and to the very end, on the fortepiano. Contemporaries speak of his "mostly wild and fantastic piano playing". Two years before his death, the song composer and entertainer Marie Nathusius (1817–1857) heard him and noted in her diary: "What he plays are also only single harmonic movements and echoes of melodies, forms that he mechanically has in his fingers." Could this sound mechanism "steady" him inwardly?

In his early years, Hölderlin's musical experience may have been limited to chamber music, possibly the world of

Telemann's *The Faithful Music Master*, flute pieces by Johann Joachim Quantz and Carl Philipp Emanuel Bach. Later, probably in Frankfurt, Mozart may have been added; his operas were part of the repertoire in this city. He will also have heard arrangements of Mozart's music in Bad Driburg, as musical life in German spa towns was traditionally lively. In addition, the views of Wilhelm Heinse on musical aesthetics may have enriched him, too. Did he know Rossini's music, about which Hegel waxed lyrical on several occasions, even some music by Beethoven? There is no proper basis for a comparison between Hölderlin's poetry permeated by Greek *musicé* and the music of his time. In this poetry, there is a "music of speech"—a rhetorical "music" of an increasingly autonomous type of poetry (Helmut Heißenbüttel), as Kleist, a clarinet player, put it. In the great elegies and hymns, the ear encounters a speech music that is self-sufficient, which also makes its setting to music so difficult, if not superfluous. Their medium is recitation, through which the musicality of these poems is realized. This is also the reason why it is precisely those "settings" of Hölderlin's poems that are most convincing, which play around, verse after verse, paraphrasing them musically rather than trying to translate the "musical material" they contain into a different medium. Such "setting to music" assists the recitation rather than transferring the performance of the poem into another "song". Josef Matthias Hauer (1883–1959), one of the early champions of twelve-tone music, first showed what is meant by this. Inspired by the philosopher Ferdinand Ebner (1882–1931), the author of *Pneumatological Fragments* (1921), Hauer began to explore Hölderlin's poems musically at an early age. The results were the *Hölderlin* song cycles op. 6 (1914) and op. 23 (1925). Hauer's first Hölderlin cycle consists of the poems "The Good Faith", "Hyperion's Song of Destiny", "Sunset",

"Curriculum Vita". The piano accompaniment plays itself *into* the poems as it were, whereby the voice can be carried by Hölderlin's language and not vice versa. The second cycle begins with the "Evening Fantasy", which in Hauer's setting is striking for its, at times, expressive dynamics ("[…] why does the sting sleep with no one but me in its breast?"); he proceeds in a similar way with the ode "The Bound River", whereby he does not musically emphasize or embellish the anaphoric phrase "Already sounds, already it sounds in his chest" of the third verse as a "beautiful passage", but presents it as the beginning of another dynamic sequence. "Des Morgens" remains purely recitative, whereas the poem "To the Fates" shifts the rhythm to the accompaniment, but allows the voice the decisive exclamation "Once/I lived like Gods" ("Einmal/Lebt ich, wie Götter").

What about the *Hölderlin Fragments by* Hanns Eisler, which he composed between 1935 and 42, and included in his *Hollywood Songbook*? Eisler stands for a free, or as critics say: Eclectic, approach to classical texts that is characterized by tightening interventions. With regard to his Hölderlin adaptations he stated (in 1961): "Especially with Hölderlin, who overwrites—by and large, such was Schiller's reproach: Hölderlin's overabundance—I pick out what I can read today. […] But as I have said before: Brecht, for example, found Hölderlin's "deplastering" or "enlivening" useful, together with what we read of and about him today". The results are musical texts that assert a fundamental equality of poet and composer and bring them to aesthetic confluence.

While Eisler's use of the term "fragment" referred to the fragmentary nature of *his* arrangement, Wolfgang Rihm dared to set Hölderlin fragments to music in the true sense of the word (1976/77). The special feature of these settings is that they take up the openness, or more precisely: The fragmentary music, and do not carry out any deliberate compositional alienation, but rather work out the "alien[ating]" elements in the text musically. This is contrasted by the composition *3 Hölderlin-Gedichte* (2004), which is based on the poems "Apology", "Half of Life", "To Zimmern". Here, the soprano voice sings what Rihm calls the "musical surplus" of the poem, while the piano accompaniment articulates a respective "attitude" (Rihm) to the poems. Unlike Eisler's settings, this voice tends to fall silent, even if it dares to excel for a few bars.

Between Eisler and Rihm stand the neo-romantic *Four Songs after Words of Friedrich Hölderlin* (1933) by Wolfgang Fortner (1907–1987) and the (tonal) *Three Songs after Hölderlin (1944)* by Hermann Reutter (1900–1985), each of which shows the withdrawal of the voice as part of the singing. Benjamin Britten (1913–1987) also referred to his *Six Hölderlin Fragments* op. 61 (1958) in the sense of Eisler's use of the word, because these songs for a high tenor voice use complete poems, arranged by the composer. This little-known cycle has since been choreographed as a ballet by Richard Alston (2013). What is striking about these settings is the pulsating piano accompaniment as well as the floating phrasing of the tenor voice. Friedhelm Döhl's musical approach to Hölderlin fragments should also be mentioned *"… but when…"*. *9 Fragments after Hölderlin for Baritone and Piano* (1969), which at times fall back into sprechgesang, or *recitativo,* with eruptive syncopations in the piano accompaniment, which then merges into the tentative, even hesitant.

Special mention should be made of György Kurtág's composition *Hölderlin Gesänge* op. 35a (1993–1997), which uses the most economical musical means to perform a baritone voice connected to Hölderlin text segments as it seems to wrestle with itself. Sporadic interjections by wind instruments provide a special dynamic for the recitative-like singing, which treads along on the verge of silence. Numerous segments of Hölderlin's poetry are taken up by other contemporary composers like Heinz Holliger, Friedrich Cerha and György Ligeti. Their minimalist vocal surges are interspersed with a transposition of Celan's poem *Tübingen, January* (with an almost ejaculatory vocal explosion at the fantasy words "Pallaksch", "Pallaksch") and a letter from Hölderlin to his mother. This creates the impression of a text collage for baritone, seemingly intertwining with the individual vocal lines. Echoes of the evangelist's voice from oratorios cannot be overheard. Musically, and in compositional terms, perhaps even more interesting are the *Three Fantasies after Friedrich Hölderlin* for sixteen-part choir (1982) by Györgi Ligeti. More restrained dynamic moments alternate with polyvocal slurring and the isolation of voices and small vocal groups, which aspire to correspond to the fragmentation of the text fragments. At the same time, the composition insists on alternating tonal relationships, especially in the second fantasy. The third fantasy exposes the voices to a strongly repetitive rhythmic series of tensile tests (intensified by high soprano registers), which, however, revert to withdrawal and restraint.

Hans Werner Henze represents a special case in the compositional reaction to Hölderlin—he speaks of the musical "relationship to the poet's word". With the exception of Wolfgang Rihm, probably no other composer has dealt with Hölderlin's life history (especially around 1806) and the problems of editing as intensively as Henze did. In his "autobiographical notes" *Travel Songs with Bohemian Fifth* (1996), he reports that he was informed in detail about the edition plans of the *Patmos Hymn* by D.E. Sattler. We also learn about his friendship with Pierre Bertaux. Under the date 30 October 1981 he notes:

> This morning I had the idea of building one of the movements of the Seventh [Symphony] on the Bertaux's accounts of the Authenrieth Clinic in Tübingen, where Hölderlin was imprisoned from 1806 to 1807 to be brought to reason with drugs and torture machines. Something like this: an arsenal of musical compositions, which are always mixed up in different ways, there is also something piranesian about it, a bad, evil 'scherzo' with screaming, shrill laughter, trembling, pathos.

Later, he writes about the structure of the third movement of this symphony, that it is composed of "several heterogeneous cells", dreaming that Pierre Bertaux and his wife (Danielle Laroche-Bouvy) had helped him compose this "difficult part of the symphony". It seems evident that Henze regarded Hölderlin's fragmentary language as just such "heterogeneous cells", but from which artistic developments of the material can emerge. Later, he speaks of transposing a "poetic form into a musical form". Accordingly, he says, it is necessary to "invent musical forms that correspond in one way or another to one or another poetic object, thought, image, affect, shape or effect". Thus, for Henze, this work on the *Seventh Symphony*, inspired by Hölderlin, resulted in the subsequent "setting to music" of *Half of [his] Life* for symphony orchestra.

Probably the best-known musical treatment of a Hölderlin motif in postmodernism is Luigi Nono's string quartet composition *Fragmente—Stille, An Diotima* (1980). In Hölderlin's elegiac design, *An Diotima*, there are sonorous sequences that are transferred to the landscape: "[…] As in loving quarrel/A thousand swarms above the strings/A thousand fleeting tones move,/Shadows and light change in sweet melodic alternation/Over the mountains" ("[…] Wie in liebendem Streit/Über dem Saitenspiel' ein tausendfältig Gewimmel/Flüchtiger Töne sich regt,/Wandelt Schatten und Licht in süßmelodischem Wechsel/Über die Berge dahin"). Nono's composition negates these "teeming/Fleeting tones". It works with silence as a musical means, whereby individual instruments with their string voices intermittently run through this silence. "How difficult it will be again to break the silence!" Susette Gontard writes to Hölderlin. It is a silence that surrounds her and increasingly determines their love for one another. From the point of view of tradition, this silence is further intensified by the fact that Hölderlin's letters to his Diotima were lost; if one considers the sheer beauty of Susette Gontard's letters to him, which have been handed down, then one laments those which have been lost even more so. It would probably have been the most profound exchange of love letters in the German language. On his part, Luigi Nono "uses" this silence in the sense that he lets it "play", as it were, with the instruments of the quartet as a doubled duo that recalls a motif of longing with a softly pulsating pizzicato, or a final echo.

Credits with Peter Weiss or: Hölderlin/Scardanelli as Media Event

Tübingen is omnipresent when ever Hölderlin is mentioned. Because he studied there, wrote his first great poems modelled on those by Schiller, and because he lived there for more than three decades, or rather "lived on", to quote Georg Büchner's *Lenz*.

Whenever we think of Hölderlin, the river Neckar flows tenaciously, touched by weeping willows, traversed by barges, circling around a small island, reflecting the yellow tower and a swan as the emblem of this poet of poets. Even the plane tree alley along the Neckar is where we find ourselves strolling along whenever we contemplate the unfathomableness of Hölderlin's works and his curious madness; we remember how we walked there as students, carrying along with us world-shattering problems together with our own all-too human troubles, sentiments, and preoccupations.

In the summer of 1995, a staged three-hour Hölderlin text collage could be seen in Tübingen, which was performed at various "stations" along this very alley depicting scenes from his life and works. It was intended to be alarming what happened at a clumsily executed monument, dedicated to Friedrich Silcher, a once popular but mediocre Swabian poet. Erected in the crude, if not brutal, manner of the time (1941), this eyesore has not been demolished to this day. There, the episode "How F. Hölderlin was appropriated by the warriors" was staged. What happened? An SS officer shouted Hölderlin verses before a youth takes the oath to the Führer. Steel-helmed soldiers from various armies shout Hölderlin verses in a pressed rhythm in the martial style of American military academies. In the end they all fall ("Falling is the most efficient thing here", to quote Rilke again), and the commander kills Hölderlin, unbeknown to him was the effect he had on these military men.

It is not long ago that film discovered Hölderlin, and in a sophisticated way. Hermann Zschoche ventured into this material in 1984, when the German Democratic Republic began to rediscover and reassess its "classical heritage". The result was the DEFA film *Half of Life,* starring the young Ulrich Mühe as Hölderlin and Jenny Gröllmann as Susette Gontard. Two years later, this film was also released in West German cinemas and performed a kind of cultural pre-reunification. The special punch line was that years later Ulrich Mühe changed sides and played the banker Gontard in Nina Grosses's great Hölderlin film *Feuerreiter* (1998). This large cinematic artwork based on Hölderlin, with a star cast—besides Ulrich Mühe—Martin Feifel (Hölderlin), Marianne Denicourt (Susette), Ulrich Matthes (Sinclair) and Nina Hoss (Marie), shows the poet as an androgynous artist and apostle of love, but also as a victim of his time, who could not help but let his poetry get in the way of himself. Half tutor, half Orpheus, he embodies the paradox of the shy daredevil, delicately strung berserker and cultivated savage. This radical, in the service of love and poetry, develops into his own adversary, who behaves with gusto. Harald Bergmann achieved further cinematic differentiation with his trilogy *Lyrische Suite/Das untergehende Vaterland* (1992), *Hölderlin Comics* (1993/94) and *Scardanelli* (2000) as well as the documentary *Passion Hölderlin* (2003). Otto Sander, Udo Samel (who also excelled as "Franz Schubert"), Rainer Sellien, André Wilms and Walter Schmidinger test their skills with Hölderlin texts. The voices of Martin Heidegger, Tina Engels and D. E. Sattler can also be heard. Bergmann makes the texts speak through his actors; they stage themselves vocally, as it were. The voices are stage-managed. In a sense, these films should have been accompanied by Beethoven's late quartets and not by Mozart. For just like Hölderlin, Beethoven's late work, as Mauricio Kagel put it, is "anti-entertainment", and thus in its constant untimeliness absolutely necessary.

Imagine Hölderlin, a poet whose seventy-three-year life fell into two halves. Whilst the film attempts to bring life and movement into the image of a life in two halves, the portrait immobilizes him: The anonymous pencil drawing of 1786, that of Immanuel Gottlieb Nast of 1788, Franz Karl Hiemer's type-casting pastel painting of 1792 with open collar, the silhouettes, the pencil drawing of Johann Georg Schreiner and Rudolf Lohbauer of 1823, and Louise Keller's drawing of the seventy-two-year-old resident in a tower. Horst Janssen had effectively combined and reworked Hölderlin's portrait at 16 by a friend of his with Louise Keller's rendering of the poet. He captioned it: "Everything that has to become, becomes still". This "becoming still" in the picture, which has forgotten how to move, seems to Hölderlin to be just as appropriate as the incessantly walking poet of the *Wanderer-Elegy*, who repeatedly and inevitably ends up amongst his fellow countrymen who are as foreign to him as he is to them.

One knows Hölderlin's alleged exclamation when he was suspected of belonging to the circle of Jacobin revolutionaries around Isaak von Sinclair, who had planned an attack on the Württemberg sovereign: "I do not want to be a Jacobin. Vive le roi!" How cryptic was the truth concealed in this exclamation? Did Hölderlin not want to be what he had actually been? So back to the explosive question: How "political" was Hölderlin really? Peter Weiss was also moved by this question when he adapted Hölderlin's material for the stage around 1969/70. As a scenic biography, his play in two acts: *Hölderlin* was premiered in 1971 in Stuttgart, under the direction of Peter Palitzsch. It belongs in the context of his other plays *Trotsky in Exile* (1970) and *The Persecution and Murder of Jean Paul Marat,* performed by the drama group of the Hospice of Charenton under the direction of Mr. de Sade (1964); however, it can also be considered one of the precursors of the novel *Aesthetics of Resistance* (1975–1980).

Weiss, who also published under the pseudonym "Sinclair", shows in eight biographically informed picture scenes the progressive, socially conditioned deformation of Hölderlin, a poet caught up in himself, who was "so certain of the ideal revolution" that it "tore him horribly out of his context". Threatened by self-alienation and isolation, he finds himself confronted with the growing conformism of his friends Schelling and Neuffer, and no less with Hegel's alleged saturation of thought, and Hegel's alleged arrangement with the structures of power. (In so doing, Weiss perpetuated the myth of Hegel's serving the Prussian establishment. Research has since convincingly shown that the philosopher never lost his interest in the French Revolution, to the point of celebrating the 14th July until the end of his life in 1831.) Even though Sinclair remains devoted to him in every situation in life; his behaviour proves increasingly opaque. Charlotte von Kalb and Susette Gontard appear in this piece as severely emotionally damaged, whereas Charlotte's partner in Waltershausen, Wilhelmine Kirms, who is believed to have been the mother of Hölderlin's only child, is supposed to be a "representative of a future emancipation".

It is debatable whether it makes sense to show, as Weiss does, the young Karl Marx in the tower in the last scene of the conversation with Hölderlin; in any case, Weiss did not proceed in a stencil-like manner in this piece, as Hellmuth Karasek argued in his review of the premiere. At any rate, Weiss succeeded in confronting us with the clichéd images we have of these protagonists and in offering different perspectives on each of them. This perspectivation rarely has a coarsening effect. Rather, Weiss achieves subtle differentiations and provides insights, for example, into the verbal faculty of his Hölderlin. One stage direction reads: "While walking, Hölderlin first emits rhythmically humming sounds, he then gradually forms words", which often rhyme. It is precisely the temporal distance of this piece that would now benefit from effective new productions. They are overdue. For Peter Weiss' *Hölderlin has* remained unique as a stage event; and his poeto-political concern has lost little of its expressive value. The play impressively works with different levels of language, ranging from the burlesque manner of the student milieu to the logic of Hegelian sentences, from the adolescent language of Hölderlin's pupil Fritz von Kalb to Autenrieth's pseudo-analytical manner of speaking, from Sinclair's emphases to Schiller's confidence in the meaning of aesthetic education and Goethe's murmuring pragmatics. Christiane Zimmer is allowed to sway, and the choir of the Fourth Estate is allowed to measure itself against the Greek archetype and "expand Hölderlin's own vision and voice". Heinrich von Kalb would like to be a colonialist, and he strives for a corresponding linguistic register, which the bankers Bethmann and Gontard supplement with their own, as do the German-national fraternity members who pay homage to the (apparently) absent-minded Hölderlin at the tower and stage a book burning with works by French authors of the revolution.

Hölderlin by Peter Weiss unites disparate biographical approaches and, especially in the characterization of individual persons, provides idiosyncratic, or at least independent, possibilities of interpretation. It is not the Hölderlin of elegies and hymns that is presented here, but the failed re-evaluator of all values. "The idea that the Tübingen monastery, which after all became the cradle of German idealism, could also have become the cradle of the German revolution, remains a fascinating drama of ideas", Karasek remarked appropriately. In the *Hölderlin* of Peter Weiss, this playing with ideas found its stage. It proves to be a space for meaningful action in the name of a poet who despaired when he realized that his existence might have been entirely futile.

They have no use for me, Hölderlin is remembered to have said, but one thing is certain: *We* are not *they*.

Literature

Editions

Friedrich Hölderlin: Sämtliche Werke. Hg. v. Norbert von Hellingrath, Bd. 4 (Gedichte 1800-1806). 2. Aufl. Berlin 1923.
Friedrich Hölderlin: Sämtliche Werke. Historisch-kritische Ausgabe Edited by Franz Zinkernagel (1914-1926). Wallstein/ Göttingen 2020a.
Friedrich Hölderlin: Sämtliche Werke. Hg. v. Friedrich Beißner. Stuttgart 1943-1985. [Große Stuttgarter Ausgabe]
Friedrich Hölderlin: Sämtliche Werke. Historisch-kritische Ausgabe in 20 Bänden und 3 Supplementen. Hg. v. Dietrich E. Sattler. Frankfurt a.M./Basel 1975–2008 [Frankfurter Ausgabe]. (Reissued by Vittorio Klostermann Verlag. Frankfurt/ Main 2020b)
Friedrich Hölderlin: Sämtliche Werke und Briefe. Drei Bände. Hg. v. Jochen Schmidt. Frankfurt a.M. 1992. [Deutscher Klassiker Verlag]
Friedrich Hölderlin: Sämtliche Werke und Briefe. Drei Bände. Hg. v. Michael Knaupp. München 1992-1993.

Friedrich Hölderlin: Sämtliche Werke, Briefe und Dokumente in zeitlicher Folge. 12 Bände. Hg. v. Dietrich E. Sattler. München/Darmstadt 2004. [Leseausgabe auf Grundlage der Frankfurter Ausgabe]

Friedrich Hölderlin: Selected Poems and Fragments. Translated by Michael Hamburger. Edited by Jeremy Adler. With a new preface and an introduction by Michel Hamburger. Penguin Books. London 1998.

Friedrich Hölderlin: Essays and Letters. Edited and Translated with an Introduction by Jeremy Adler and Charlie Louth. Penguin Books. London 2009.

Friedrich Hölderlin: Hyperion or The Hermit in Greece. Translated by India Russell. Melrose Books. Ely 2016.

Friedrich Hölderlin: Selected Poems and Letters. Translated by Christopher Middleton. The Last Books. Amsterdam 2019.

Documents

Friedrich Hölderlin. Eine Chronik in Text und Bild. Hg. v. Adolf Beck und Paul Raabe. Frankfurt a.M. 1970a.

Hölderlin. Eine Ausstellung zum 200. Geburtstag. Katalog hg. v. Werner Volke. Marbach am Neckar 1970b.

Friedrich Hölderlin. Dichter über ihre Dichtungen Bd. 11. Hg. v. Friedrich Beißner. München 1973.

Hölderlin im Turm. Marbacher Magazin 11/1978. Bearbeitet von Werner Volke. Marbach am Neckar 1979.

Beckermann, Thomas/Canaris, Volker (Hg.): Der andere Hölderlin: Materialien. Frankfurt a.M. 1972.

Härtling, Peter/Kurz, Gerhard (Hg.): Hölderlin und Nürtingen. Stuttgart 1994.

Hornbogen, Helmut: Die Tübinger Platanenallee. Mit einem Vorwort von Hermann Bausinger und einem Nachwort von Wilfried Setzler. Tübingen 2007.

Ueding, Gert (Hg.): Tübingen. Ein Städte-Lesebuch. Frankfurt a.M. 1990.

Resources

Wörterbuch zu Friedrich Hölderlin. I. Teil: Die Gedichte. Auf der Textgrundlage der Großen Stuttgarter Ausgabe. Bearbeitet von Heinz-Martin Dannhauer und Klaus Schuffels. Tübingen 1983.
Wörterbuch zu Friedrich Hölderlin. II. Teil: Hyperion. Auf der Textgrundlage der Großen Stuttgarter Ausgabe. Bearbeitet von Hans Otto Horch, Klaus Schuffels, Manfred Kammer. Tübingen 1992.

Anthological

Gnüg, Hiltrud (Hg.): An Hölderlin. Zeitgenössische Gedichte. Stuttgart 1993.
Kermani, Navid (Hg.): Bald sind wir aber Gesang. Ausgewählte Gedichte Friedrich Hölderlins. München 2020.
Kurz, Gerhard (Hg.): Gedichte von Friedrich Hölderlin. Interpretationen. Stuttgart 1996a.
Reich-Ranicki, Marcel (Hg.): Friedrich Hölderlin "Und voll mit wilden Rosen". 33 Gedichte mit Interpretationen. Mit einem Vorwort von Peter von Matt. Frankfurt a.M. und Leipzig 2009.

Research Overviews

Hölderlin-Jahrbuch. Begründet von Friedrich Beißner und Paul Kluckhohn. Im Auftrag der Hölderlin-Gesellschaft herausgegeben von Sabine Doering, Michael Franz und Martin Vöhler. Tübingen 2015. (Derzeit im 39. Band, erscheint alle zwei Jahre.)
Arnold, Heinz Ludwig (Hg.): Friedrich Hölderlin. Text + Kritik. Sonderband. München 1996.
Beyer, Uwe (Hg.): Neue Wege zu Hölderlin. Würzburg 1994.

Hieber, Jochen: Der Höhepunkt des Hölderlinjahrs. In: Frankfurter Allgemeine Zeitung of 26 July, 2020.
Jamme, Christoph/Schneider, Helmut (Hg.): Mythologie der Vernunft. Hegels „ältestes Systemprogramm des deutschen Idealismus". Frankfurt a.M. 1988.
Jamme, Christoph/Pöggeler, Otto (Hg.): Homburg vor der Höhe in der deutschen Geistesgeschichte. Stuttgart 1981.
Kurz, Gerhard/Lawitschka, Valerie/Wertheimer, Jürgen (Hg.): Hölderlin und die Moderne. Eine Bestandsaufnahme. Tübingen 1995.
Lange, Wolfgang/Schmidt, Jochen: Das Wahnsinns-Projekt oder was es mit einer "antiempedokleischen Wendung" im Spätwerk Hölderlins auf sich hat/Stellungnahme. In: Deutsche Vierteljahrsschrift für Literaturwissenschaft und Geistesgeschichte 63(1989), Heft 4, 645-714.
Riedel, Ingrid (Hg.): Hölderlin ohne Mythos. Göttingen 1973a.
Louth, Charlie: Urge fort he impossible. 250 years oft he complex, necessary Friedrich Hölderlin. In: Times Literary Supplement of 13 November, 2020, p. 28-29.
Roberg, Thomas (Hg.): Friedrich Hölderlin. Neue Wege der Forschung. Darmstadt ²2007a.

Biographical Information

Amette, Jacques-Pierre: Le voyage de Hölderlin en France. Paris 1991.
Beißner, Friedrich (Hrsg.): Dichter über ihre Dichtungen: Friedrich Hölderlin. München 1973.
Bertaux, Pierre: Friedrich Hölderlin. Eine Biographie. Frankfurt a.M./Leipzig 2000.
Burdorf, Dieter: Friedrich Hölderlin. München 2011.
Brauer, Ursula: Hölderlin und Susette Gontard. Eine Liebesgeschichte. Hamburg 2002.
Gaier, Ulrich: Hölderlin. Eine Einführung. Tübingen/Basel 1993.

Ivanovic, Christine: "Bereit, an übrigem Orte". Hölderlins, Winkel von Hahrdt' als Erinnerungsort. Spuren 79. Marbach am Neckar 2009.
Härtling, Peter: Hölderlin. Ein Roman. Darmstadt/Neuwied ²1980.
Michel, Wilhelm: Das Leben Friedrich Hölderlins. Bremen 1940.
Knubben, Thomas: Hölderlin. Eine Winterreise. Tübingen 2011.
Langner, Beatrix: Hölderlin und Diotima. Eine Biographie. Frankfurt a.M. 2001.
Link, Jürgen: Hölderlins Fluchtlinie Griechenland. Vandenhoeck & Ruprecht. Göttingen 2020.
Martens, Gunter: Friedrich Hölderlin. Reinbek b. Hamburg 1996.
Merlio, Gilbert/Pelletier, Nicole (Hg.): Bordeaux au temps de Hölderlin. Bern u.a. 1997.
Ott, Karl-Heinz: Hölderlins Geister. München 2019.
Safranski, Rüdiger: Hölderlin. Komm! Ins Offene, Freund!. München 2019.
Schünemann, Peter: Scardanellis Gedächtnis. München 2007.
Waiblinger, Wilhelm: Friedrich Hölderlins Leben, Dichtung und Wahnsinn. In: Ders., Mein flüchtiges Glück. Tagebücher, Briefe, Prosa. Hg. v. Wolfgang Hartwig. Berlin 1991, S. 283-318.
Weiss, Peter: Hölderlin. Stück in zwei Akten. Neufassung. Frankfurt a.M. 1971.

Research Literature

Adorno, Theodor W.: Parataxis. Zur späten Lyrik Hölderlins. In: Ders., Noten zur Literatur. Gesammelte Schriften Bd. 11. Hg. v. Rolf Tiedemann unter Mitwirkung von Gretel Adorno, Susan Buck-Morss und Klaus Schultz. Frankfurt a.M. 1974, 447-491.
Binder, Wolfgang: Friedrich Hölderlin. Hg. v. Elisabeth Binder und Klaus Weimar. Frankfurt a.M. 1987.
Bennholdt-Thomson, Anke/Guzzoni, Alfredo: Analecta Hölderliana. Zur Hermetik des Spätwerks. Würzburg 1999.

Borio, Gianmario/Polledri, Elena (Eds.): „Wechsel der Töne". Musikalische Elemente in Friedrich Hölderlins Dichtung und ihre Rezeption bei den Komponisten. Heidelberg 2019.
Bothe, Henning: "Ein Zeichen sind wir, deutungslos". Die Rezeption Hölderlins von ihren Anfängen bis zu Stefan George. Stuttgart 1992.
Cooper, Ian: The Near and Distant God. Poetry, Idealism and Religious Thought from Hölderlin to Eliot. London 2008.
Doering, Sabine: Aber was ist diß? Formen und Funktionen der Frage in Hölderlins dichterischem Werk. Göttingen 1992.
Görner, Rüdiger: Hölderlins Mitte. Zur Ästhetik eines Ideals. München 1993.
Haverkamp, Anselm: Laub voll Trauer: Hölderlins spate Allegorie. München 1991.
Haverkamp, Anselm: Leaves of Mourning. Hölderlin's Late Work. With an Essay on Keats and Melancholy. Transl. By Vernon Chadwick. New York 1996.
Heidegger, Martin: Erläuterungen zu Hölderlins Dichtung. Frankfurt a.M. ^{5}1981.
Henrich, Dieter: Der Grund im Bewußtsein. Untersuchungen zu Hölderlins Denken (1794-1795). Stuttgart 1992.
Henrich, Dieter: Sein oder Nichts. Erkundungen um Samuel Beckett und Hölderlin. München 2016.
Hoffmeister, Johannes: Hölderlin und Hegel. Tübingen 1931.
Lernout, Geert: The Poet as Thinker: Hölderlin in France. Columbia 1994.
Linke, Detlef B.: Hölderlin als Hirnforscher. Frankfurt a.M. 2005.
Nägele, Rainer: Hölderlins Kritik der poetischen Vernunft. Basel 2005.
Kaiser, Corinna: Gustav Landauer als Schriftsteller: Sprache, Schweigen, Musik. Berlin/Boston 2014.
Kocziszky, Éva: Mythenfiguren in Hölderlins Spätwerk, Würzburg 1997.
Kocziszky, Éva: Hölderlins Orient, Würzburg 2009.
Kocziszky, Éva (Hg.): Wozu Dichter? Hundert Jahre Poetologien nach Hölderlin. Berlin 2016.

Kreuzer, Johann (Hrsg.): Hölderlin-Handbuch. Leben—Werk—Wirkung. Stuttgart 2020.
Kurz, Gerhard: Mittelbarkeit und Vereinigung. Stuttgart 1975.
Kurz, Gerhard (Hrsg.): Gedichte von Friedrich Hölderlin. Interpretationen. Stuttgart 1996b.
Menninghaus, Winfried: Hälfte des Lebens. Versuch über Hölderlins Poetik. Frankfurt a.M. 2005.
Mieth, Günter: Friedrich Hölderlin: Zeit und Schicksal. Vorträge 1962-2006. Würzburg 2007.
Ogden, Mark: The Problem of Christ in the Work of Friedrich Hölderlin. London 1991.
Riedel, Ingrid (Hrsg.): Hölderlin ohne Mythos. Göttingen 1973b.
Roberg, Thomas (Hrsg.): Friedrich Hölderlin. Neue Wege der Forschung. Darmstadt 2007b.
Schmidt, Jochen: Hölderlins geschichtsphilosophische Hymnen 'Friedensfeier' – 'Der Einzige' – 'Patmos'. Darmstadt 1990.
Stefa, Niketa: Die Entgegensetzung in Hölderlins Poetologie. Würzburg 2011.
Wegenast, Margarethe: Hölderlins Spinoza-Rezeption und ihre Bedeutung für die Konzeption des 'Hyperion'. Tübingen 1990.

Other Sources

Atik, Anne: Wie es war. Erinnerungen an Samuel Beckett. Aus dem Englischen übersetzt von Wolfgang Held. Frankfurt a.M. 2003.
Beckett, Samuel: Trötentöne/Mirlitonnades. Französisch und deutsch. Übertragen von Barbara Köhler. Frankfurt a.M. 2005.
Bollack, Jean: Paul Celan. Poetik der Fremdheit. Wien 2000.
Danz, Daniela: Das philosophische Licht um mein Fenster. Über Friedrich Hölderlin. Stiftung Lyrik-Kabinett München 2016.
Engels, Matthias/Kade, Thomas/Trelenberg, Thorsten (Hrsg.): Hölderlinks. Türme, Wolkenkratzer, Wohngebäude. Hölderlin in 73 lyrischen, dokumentarischen, prosaischen Stücken zum Zusammensetzen. Bochum/Freiburg 2020.

Filer, Nathan: The Heartland. Finding and losing schizophrenia. London 2019.

Fischer-Seidel, Therese/Fries-Dieckmann, Marion: Der unbekannte Beckett: Samuel Beckett und die deutsche Kultur. Frankfurt a.M. 2005.

Gascoyne, David: Selected Poems. Enitharmon Press 1994.

Gfrereis, Heike: Hölderlin, Celan und die Sprache der Poesie. Exhibition Catalogue. Marbach/Neckar 2020.

Henze, Hans Werner: Reiselieder mit böhmischen Quinten. Autobiographische Mitteilungen 1926-1995. Frankfurt a.M. 1996.

Jaspers, Karl: Strindberg and van Gogh. A comparative analysis with reference to Swedenborg and Hölderlin. Translated by Oskar Grunow and David Woloshin. University of Arizona Press 1977.

Rakusa, Ilma: Corona mit Hölderlin. In: manuskripte 60(2020), 228, pp. 5-13.

Trakl, Georg, Hölderlin. In: Weichselbaum, Hans: Unbekannte Gedichte und Prosa Georg Trakls entdeckt. In: Degner, Uta/ Weichselbaum, Hans/ Wolf, Norbert Christian (Hrsg.): Autorschaft und Poetik in Texten und Kontexten Georg Trakls. Salzburg 2016, pp. 405-424.

GPSR Compliance
The European Union's (EU) General Product Safety Regulation (GPSR) is a set of rules that requires consumer products to be safe and our obligations to ensure this.

If you have any concerns about our products, you can contact us on

ProductSafety@springernature.com

In case Publisher is established outside the EU, the EU authorized representative is:

Springer Nature Customer Service Center GmbH
Europaplatz 3
69115 Heidelberg, Germany

www.ingramcontent.com/pod-product-compliance
Ingram Content Group UK Ltd.
Pitfield, Milton Keynes, MK11 3LW, UK
UKHW021251180426
11946UKWH00004B/72